PLATO'S *R*

Continuum Reader's Guides

PLATO'S *REPUBLIC*

A Reader's Guide

LUKE PURSHOUSE

continuum

Continuum International Publishing Group
The Tower Building   80 Maiden Lane
11 York Road   Suite 704
London SE1 7NX   New York, NY 10038

British Library Cataloguing-in-Publication Data
A catalogue record for this book is available from the British Library.

ISBN: 0826474667 (hardback) 0826474675 (paperback)

Library of Congress Cataloguing-in-Publication Data
A catalog record for this book is available from the Library of Congress.

Typeset by Servis Filmsetting Ltd, Manchester
Printed and bound in Great Britain by Ashford Colour Press Ltd,
Gosport, Hampshire

CONTENTS

CHAPTER 1

CONTEXT

1.1. PLATO AND SOCRATES

Plato was born in Athens in 427 BC, into a family of wealth and long-standing political influence. He is said to have been a personable young man of great physical attractiveness, a skilled wrestler as well as a talented artistic writer, besides ranking among the greatest philosophers the world has known. Indeed, given his talents and lineage, Plato might well have been expected to play a key role in the political life of his city. However, due to a number of factors, perhaps most significantly the death of his revered teacher and friend Socrates, he was to become increasingly disillusioned with what he saw as the violence and corruption attendant on the Athenian democracy in which he lived. Indeed, his opposition to this system was a key tenet of his thought, as we shall see in the *Republic*.

As Plato rejected active political life, he sought an answer for society's problems in philosophy instead. To this end, he travelled, taught and advised extensively, writing more than 20 Philosophical Dialogues. In addition, he founded the Academy in Athens early in the fourth century BC, which was one of the first permanent institutions for philosophical education, and a precursor of the Western university system. In one form or another, this establishment existed for over 900 years, and even in Plato's time numbered many men of intellectual influence among its pupils. Most famously, these included Aristotle, a native of Stageira, who settled in Athens as Plato's disciple. He was to become a philosopher and scientist of encyclopaedic range, who would dominate medieval European thought, and who counted among his own pupils such politically significant figures as Alexander the Great.

Plato himself did not, however, remain in Athens throughout his life. He made as many as three extended trips to Syracuse, to the court of the tyrant ruler Dionysios, and later as an adviser to his son. His first visit ended in disaster, when he incurred Dionysios' wrath by arguing against his ruthless and autocratic system of government and his private life of debauched excess. Dionysios reputedly had Plato sold into slavery, from which he had to be purchased back into freedom by a sympathetic philosopher. Astonishingly, Plato was nonetheless persuaded to return to Syracuse after the tyrant's death, to act as philosophical mentor to the weaker and less competent, but equally autocratic and debauched, younger Dionysios. Their relationship was again an uneasy one; the young ruler evinced a keen interest in Plato's moral and philosophical precepts, but proved unwilling or unable to put them into practice. Indeed, Plato may have been fortunate to escape his last visit to Syracuse with his life – shortly after his departure Dionysios was overthrown in a violent rebellion, and lived out the remainder of his days in relative obscurity. Plato himself returned to Athens, where he died of natural causes (aged 80) in 347 BC.

The young Plato's relationship with Socrates was clearly a formative influence on his philosophy. For all his fame and influence, however, nothing we know of Socrates comes to us through his own writing. Indeed, although other sources, notably Xenophon, offer different perspectives on Socrates' life and teaching, the majority of what we learn comes from the works of Plato. Thus, the Socrates we 'know' is essentially Plato's depiction, or even Plato's creation, leading to near-insoluble difficulties for anyone who wishes to discuss the two philosophers in isolation.

We gather that Socrates was a one-time soldier, famous for feats of prodigious physical endurance, who was to attract a wide and devoted following among the young, rich Athenian intelligentsia, prior to his execution in 399 BC. While he may have eschewed wealth, often advertising the fact that he did not charge for his teaching, he did not eschew the wealthy, and sophisticated dinner-parties (*symposia*) were a commonplace of his lifestyle, and the setting for some of Plato's dialogues. Socrates' family, however, dwelt in comparative poverty.

Socrates' favoured form of teaching famously relied upon questioning rather than instructing in order to enable his pupils to arrive, through guidance, at a conclusion through their own intellectual efforts. Socrates' teaching technique is at the heart of the literary form which Plato pioneered as a vehicle to showcase Socrates', and his own, ideas: the Philosophical Dialogue. This style of writing, at once literary and philosophical, drew heavily on dramatic traditions, taking the form of a kind of script, with arguments delivered as if from the mouths of different characters. Many of Plato's works used this form, though admittedly he also employed a more narrative, prose-based style for those texts involving more characters or more complex activity, such as the *Protagoras* and *Symposium*.

As mentioned earlier, Socrates' death was perhaps the most important single factor in influencing Plato's increasing hostility to the society in which he lived. Socrates was prosecuted in 399 BC, officially on two counts: impiety, or more specifically the introduction of new divine powers, and corruption of the Athenian youth. These accusations may well have been a smokescreen for a more political charge, as Socrates was well-known for criticizing his city's government and institutions, and had links to the leadership of a brief Spartan-imposed despotic coup carried out by 'The Thirty' in 404 BC. He was, in any case, convicted and put to a horrible death, being made to drink hemlock; Plato himself was present at the execution. It seems likely that the jurors at the trial were prejudiced against Socrates from the outset, though the philosopher's mismanagement of his own defence was also to his disadvantage. For, while Plato, in the *Apology*, portrays him speaking eloquently if somewhat fatalistically, other sources show his presenting a more bumbling account of himself, and it is generally agreed that, when asked to nominate a suitable punishment for the jury to vote on, he arrogantly suggested that his penalty should be to receive a financial allowance from the state.

Socrates figures as the central character in most of Plato's dialogues, where his depiction is testimony to the immense regard the author afforded him. He is invariably portrayed, not only as a more adept philosopher than his interlocutors, but as an essentially good man, committed to truth, learning, and teaching, unmindful of wealth and other material goods, and a force for reason and virtue in a world where many pursue much less high-minded goals. Nowhere is this clearer than in the *Republic*, where he figures as the advocate of the ethical life, pitted against those who urge the pursuit of riches, pleasure and power. Before turning in detail to this work, however, I shall offer a brief summary of Plato's philosophical writings, and say something of the social backdrop against which the *Republic* was written.

1.2. PLATO'S WRITINGS

It is difficult to trace a precise chronology for Plato's works, as none is dated, and relevant contemporary sources are sparse. Indeed, there are certain texts which have traditionally been credited to Plato, for example the *Epinomis*, *Hippias Major* and *Epistles*, over whose authenticity there is considerable doubt. The works whose attribution to Plato is more certain number in the mid-twenties, and their approximate chronology has been established by scholars, largely by tracing the development of the author's philosophical theory and literary style.

Plato's early dialogues are largely homogenous in terms of structure. Each typically consists of one or more characters' attempts to define a single central concept, definitions which are then tested by Socrates and invariably shown to be mistaken or incoherent. The concepts dealt with in these dialogues are mostly ethical or related to human conduct: the *Laches* concerns courage, the *Euthyphro* piety, the *Charmides* temperance, the *Lysis* friendship and the *Protagoras* (probably the latest of these) virtue as a whole. The conclusions of these dialogues, moreover, are essentially negative; certain attempts at definition are refuted by Socrates, but he offers no alternative 'correct' accounts with which to replace them. Indeed, he frequently professes himself to be ignorant of the true nature of the concepts involved, confining his project to the demonstration that those who believe themselves to have knowledge of them actually do not.

The dialogues from Plato's middle period exhibit more variety of structure, and generally greater subtlety of argument, than his earlier works. The *Gorgias*, some of whose themes foreshadow those of the *Republic* itself, sees Socrates actively defending the life of virtue and philosophic contemplation against a lively and determined opponent called Callicles, who advocates instead the pursuit of sensual pleasure and political power. The *Meno* also presents Socrates as propounding his own views, in this case concerning, among other topics, the process by which human beings acquire knowledge; a precursor to the more detailed discussions of education and epistemology contained in the *Republic*.

It is significant that although the *Republic* is generally regarded as a middle- to late-period work, the first of its ten books bear many hallmarks of an early Socratic Dialogue. The moral concept discussed, in this case, is justice (*dikaiosunē*), and as in the early works Socrates spends most of the discussion thwarting the efforts of his interlocutors, Cephalus, Polemachus and Thrasymachus, to provide adequate accounts of this notion. The book ends, moreover, with Socrates admitting that he cannot sensibly comment on the value of justice, as he is unable to say what justice is (354b–c). He thus offers no positive teaching on his subject-matter; rather, as in the early dialogues, he simply undermines the claims of others.

The beginning of the *Republic* Book II, however, ushers in a marked change both in literary style and philosophical endeavour. Two brothers, Glaucon and Adeimantus, make lengthy speeches which challenge Socrates to explain why justice is a quality worth having in a human life. Socrates' answer leads him via a lengthy exposition of the nature of justice, both as a quality of a political community and an individual human being; and seminal discourses on a range of tangentially related issues, summarized below in Chapter 2. Moreover, from the middle of Book II (368a) to the end of the *Republic*, the work becomes a virtual monologue conducted through Socrates, with the roles of other characters being mostly limited to affirming his points without question. Apart from some occasional questions and interjections, for example by Polemachus and Adeimantus in Books V (449a–450a) and VI (487a), Socrates is allowed free rein to develop a detailed and subtly interwoven set of arguments, leading ultimately to his conclusion in Book IX (580b–c) that a just life is far happier and more pleasant than one of injustice.

There is some possibility, given the marked difference of style between Book I and the rest of the *Republic*, that the first book was written earlier, and existed for a while as a self-contained dialogue outlining the problems, as Plato saw them, with certain contemporary accounts of justice. It is indeed conceivable that Plato wrote the remainder of the *Republic* as a later attempt to address the important questions – also treated in the *Gorgias* – which Book I left unanswered; namely, what is justice, and why if at all should we adopt it. Socrates' brief attempts in the first book to convert Thrasymachus to the cause of being just are notably unconvincing, so the subsequent books may thus be seen as seeking to offer a more discursive, and ultimately more persuasive, treatment of this issue.

Although probably the most famous of Plato's works, the *Republic* was not his last. Among his later writings are the *Timaeus* and *Parmenides*, which address mainly metaphysical issues, and the *Philebus*, which is concerned with the relative desirability of wisdom and pleasure, affirming the clear superiority, in Plato's view, of the former, and thereby revisiting an area explored in *Republic* IX. The *Theaetetus*, another later writing, is generally regarded as Plato's greatest epistemological work; while its form again recalls those of early dialogues in that it offers no positive answer to its central question – 'what is knowledge?' – the sophistication of its arguments testifies to its relative maturity.

The dialogue believed to be Plato's last is the *Laws* – a political text, and unusual insofar as the central didactic role is occupied not by Socrates, but by an unnamed 'Athenian'. It is instructive to compare the constitutional and social policies advocated in the *Laws* with those in the political sections of the *Republic*. While some of the *Republic*'s proposals, for instance concerning the abolition of the family and censorship of the arts, reappear in the later work, the *Laws* is in other ways less radical in its demands for societal restructuring. Certain democratic institutions are admitted, not as ideal, but as pragmatic second-best arrangements, whereas the *Republic* had called for their abolition. Perhaps in writing the *Laws*, the older Plato wanted to outline what he regarded as the best political system achievable in practice, as opposed to the perfectly just but possibly too idealistic and unfeasible arrangements the *Republic* proposed.

1.3. SOCIAL AND POLITICAL BACKGROUND

The *Republic* is strongly rooted in the Athenian society in which Plato lived. As we shall see, several important elements of Athens' social and political structures are subjected to severe criticism in the dialogue, and it is important to be aware of this context to appreciate the contemporary significance of Plato's arguments.

Athens was famed for its radical democratic system of government, with a very high degree of involvement for the 'ordinary' citizen in the institutions of state – far higher, indeed, than in virtually all of today's democratic societies. It is difficult, in historical terms, to identify a clear beginning of Athens' democratic system. A voting assembly of Athenian citizens (*ekklēsia*) had formally existed since at least the time of Solon (594–561 BC). However, it was Kleisthenes in 508–7 who introduced reforms which began to shape Athens into the democracy Plato would have recognized. Under this constitution, all national decisions were dealt with first by the Presidents (*prutaneis*) and the Council of Five

Hundred (*boulē*), both of whose members were chosen randomly by lot. They were then passed, if deemed sufficiently important, to an Assembly, which citizens were paid to attend. Participation in the democracy was available to all freeborn male citizens of any social class, provided they could prove that they were of good Athenian stock. These people also had the right to act as jurors in what was a notoriously litigious society. Excluded were slaves and freedmen, immigrants and their families – among whom Aristotle, a Macedonian, was counted – and all classes of women. Thus, at around 431 BC, shortly after Plato's birth, it is estimated that out of around 300,000–350,000 people living within the geographical boundaries of Athens, only about 50,000 had full citizenship rights.[1]

Athenians were far from united in approving of their political system. The Assembly was notoriously fickle and easily swayed by demagogues, of whom Cleon and Pericles are perhaps the best known. Still, with the exception of two brief interruptions towards the end of the fifth century BC, democracy in Athens was a stable system of government, existing in some form for almost 200 years. The eventual closing-down of the democratic state, moreover, was precipitated not by forces or dissatisfactions within the city itself but by the invasion of Sparta, a neighbouring, non-democratic military power.

A second major element of Athenian society, which the *Republic* addresses at length, is the importance of poetry, in particular the epic poems accredited to Homer. These works, which recounted supposedly historical events of the fourteenth century BC such as the Fall of Troy, intermingled with stories of gods, monsters and sorcery, were passed down through an oral tradition, becoming texts by (at the latest) the end of the sixth century. Little is known of the historical Homer; indeed, it is doubtful whether any such person existed. The Athenians, however, believed that he did, and the major Homeric works, the *Iliad* and the *Odyssey*, occupied an immensely prominent position in Athenian culture, theology and indeed ethics. Homer formed the major part of the literary and moral education of Athenian youth, and knowledge of his works was commonly seen as conferring academic prestige upon a citizen. At the same time, the poetry was rendered accessible to the general public, with poems being recited aloud by professional orators (called rhapsodes), often with musical accompaniment, at numerous venues throughout the city. Such performances were particularly commonplace at festivals, foremost among which was the Great Panathenaea festival, held in

Athens once every four years, at which both the *Iliad* and *Odyssey* were ritually performed in full.

Homeric epic poetry, which mixed history and myth, human and divine in a similar fashion to the Old Testament, probably led to a blurring of the distinction between truth and fiction in the minds of many Athenians. The poems' accounts and stories of the gods, and their interventions in human affairs, were widely regarded as having theological authority, and formed the basis of much Athenian religious belief. Likewise, the tales of heroic deeds by Odysseus and others were not only taken as grounded in fact, but were extremely influential in moulding Athenian social mores, with the Homeric hero considered an ideal to which soldiers and citizens should aspire. The values promoted by Homer, often emphasizing the military virtues of bravery and resourcefulness and the importance of receiving public acclaim for one's deeds, are, we shall see, very different from those espoused by Plato.

A third feature of Plato's contemporary Athenian culture, which is highly relevant to the *Republic*'s arguments, is the way in which philosophy was practised in the city, in particular by a prominent group of (mostly foreign) teachers known as the Sophists. This group, which counted among their number Protagoras and Hippias, as well as Thrasymachus who is lampooned in *Republic* I, offered education to wealthy young Athenians in return for considerable sums of money. As there are very few surviving Sophistic writings, and most of our knowledge of them comes from their opponents, it is difficult to divine any characteristic 'school of thought' to which they consistently adhered. They appear, for the most part, to have been moral sceptics, seeking to undermine conventional ideas of what is good and right. As Plato presents it, however, much of their teaching concerned debating style rather than philosophical substance. They trained their pupils in rhetorical persuasive techniques and clever verbal trickery of a kind that might enable one to 'win' arguments by outwitting or bamboozling one's opponents. Such skills may have been useful to young noblemen pursuing careers in politics or law, who sought to manipulate the moods of audiences to their own advantage. For Plato, however, the Sophists had lost sight of philosophy's main purpose, namely the discovery of truth. Not only did he therefore treat them with notable contempt, but he sought to distance their aims, methods and practices as far as possible from those of Socrates, a distinction strongly upheld in the *Republic*.[2]

CHAPTER 2

OVERVIEW OF THEMES

The standard English title of Plato's text – *Republic* – is of Latin origin; the original Greek title was *Politeia*, which most closely translates as meaning a political constitution or regime. The topics covered in the work, however, include not only political and social organization but a huge variety: from ethics, through human psychology, education, epistemology, the nature of philosophy and the arts to the afterlife, to name but some. The core issue is justice, a notion which is explored in two different contexts in the course of Plato's discussions. This chapter will comprise a brief synopsis of the *Republic*'s main line of argument and a survey of some of its principal themes, which serve as an introduction to the more detailed exegesis and criticism of specific passages found in Chapter 3.

2.1. TWO NOTIONS OF JUSTICE

The first context is justice understood as a quality, or virtue, of an individual human being. What does it mean, Plato asks, for someone to be just or lead a just life? Moreover, is the life of justice a desirable one, or do we make ourselves better off by being unjust? The second context is political. What sort of constitutional arrangements are required for justice in a state? How do we go about establishing and sustaining a just system of government? And how and why do certain societies fail to achieve justice?

The focus of argument throughout the *Republic* fluctuates between the levels of the individual soul (*psuchē*) and the state (*polis*). Plato begins by addressing the nature of justice as a quality of an individual. In Book I, we encounter a somewhat unpleasant character called Thrasymachus, based on the contemporary Sophist of this name, who argues with Socrates about the value of living in accordance with justice. Thrasymachus claims that the happiest life is attained by someone who manages to be as unjust as possible with impunity – the best example is a tyrant who rules a state corruptly for his own advantage. Such a person, Thrasymachus suggests, benefits from the large scale exploitation of others, enjoying individual power, wealth and pleasure at other citizens' expense. Socrates, however, disagrees that the tyrant's life is desirable and instead proposes an opposite view; namely that justice, rather than injustice, most tends to an agent's advantage.

In Book II, Socrates is challenged to defend this position, which he is told runs counter to popular opinion. His response is to take a step back, saying that until the nature of justice has been adequately defined, it is impossible to say whether being just is, or is not, in one's interest. To understand what justice is, moreover, we should first examine it within the context of a political state, where it operates on a larger scale than in a single human being. Once it is seen in this magnified context, an analogous account may be given of justice in the individual. Following this route, Socrates examines, in a section overlapping from Book II to Book IV, the essence of a political community, and the sorts of institutions and organizational principles which might render it just. Justice, he argues, obtains when everyone within a state carries out the function most appropriate to their abilities and training. In particular, the state should be governed by the class of people most fitted and best educated for the task. Its 'guardians', in other words, should be people of outstanding calibre who have undergone rigorous programmes of mental and physical preparation for this most important role.

Having established his account of political justice, Plato turns, as promised, in Book IV, to argue by analogy to the nature of justice in an individual soul. This, he claims, involves the same principle as political justice, namely that each component part of the whole entity fulfils its allotted task. In a human soul, it is the role of reason (*logos*), to take charge of the emotions and appetites, to determine ends and make choices regarding action. The just person is thus characterized as someone in whom reason and rationality are predominant, and whose non-rational desires are kept under careful restraint. For Plato, such a state of character implies psychic health and good order: since reason is the part of us best suited to exercise control and make decisions, it follows that the person who is predominantly rational has a well-arranged and orderly psychology. Someone whose passions and appetites dictate their conduct, by contrast, is mentally disordered and governed by an inferior part of their psyche. The desirability of the just life, on Plato's account, stems largely from this view that justice is akin to health and injustice to disease: a just person is one whose soul is properly ordered, while unjust people suffer from a perverse and topsy-turvy psychological makeup.

In Book V, the pendulum swings back to the analysis of political justice. Socrates is asked again about the constitution of his ideal state, and consequently engages in detailed discussions of the role of women and the family, and, most significantly, advances the proposal that the state's ruling class should consist of trained philosophers. This view leads him to discourse further upon the character and education of the 'true philosopher', someone whom he not only deems essential for the just state, but who also embodies his conception of individual justice. The analysis of both species of justice are further supplemented, in Books VIII and IX, with outlines of various types of *in*justice which can exist in states or in human personalities; the last of which, 'tyranny', is the most extremely unjust known to man. Someone whose soul is 'tyrannical', Socrates claims, lives the most wretched of lives, suffering friendlessness, discontent and enslavement to the basest elements of his own psyche. By thus inverting Thrasymachus's view that the life of a tyrant is the best life possible, Socrates reiterates his view that the more just one's soul, the better and happier one's existence.

2.2. CRITICISMS OF ATHENIAN SOCIETY

If justice, and the value of a just life, is the central theme of the *Republic*, its presentation is interspersed with seminal treatises on a range of other philosophical and political topics. Although many of these relate to issues of enduring concern, the work is notably grounded in Plato's own Athenian culture, and incorporates a number of thinly disguised attacks on contemporary institutions and practices. Foremost among these is the Athenian democracy itself.

Plato's strongest objection to the politics of his native city was the involvement in government of people who, in his judgement, lacked the knowledge, ability and training to rule well. According to *Republic* Book VI, anyone wishing to take a leading role in a democratic society is forced to tailor their ideas to the preferences and moods of the ignorant majority, rather than using their expertise to decide on the best policies for the overall good of the state. Plato contrasts such a system, where the uninformed and unruly masses exert control over government, with his utopia in which an elite group of virtuous philosophers has unassailable control over policy-making. This group, he argues, can employ their intellectual acumen and understanding of ethical truths to craft a good society, whose members willingly submit to rule by those whom they acknowledge as intellectually and morally superior.

Plato thus advocates a *meritocracy* in place of the political egalitarianism fashionable in his city. He returns to this subject in Book VIII, engaging in a vicious satire of democratic society, portraying it as an anarchic nightmare world where no respect is given to knowledge, experience, age or indeed the law; where no kinds of rank or hierarchy are acknowledged and where convicted criminals and animals roam the streets. Indeed, democracy is ranked as the second-worst of all political constitutions – only tyranny, Plato thinks, is worse. Largely, no doubt, his opposition to the Athenian democracy was motivated by its treatment of his mentor Socrates, though his own aristocratic background might also have played its part, and it is noteworthy that his cousin Critias was one of 'The Thirty', mentioned in section 1.3, who briefly governed Athens following an oligarchic coup.

There are other elements of Athenian society which receive short shrift from Plato. The established literary canon, comprising Homer and other tragic poets, he condemns both as morally corrupting and misleading about important matters of fact, not least concerning religion. Such poetry is, Plato argues, sufficiently dangerous to warrant censorship, especially for the young who are being trained for leading positions in the city. The *Republic* contains two passages devoted to the arts: the first, spanning the end of Book II and opening of Book III, focuses on their role in education; with the second, in Book X, comprising a more general critique. While cognisant of the power of literature and other art forms to influence beliefs and behaviour, Plato is pessimistic about art's capacity to be a force for good. In particular, he thinks artists lack the knowledge, most importantly the knowledge of ethics, needed to educate leading citizens and promote their moral development. Moreover, artistic work tends to appeal to what Plato regards as lower parts of the soul – the passions and sentiments – rather than reason. The superiority of philosophy over fictional literature, as a source of learning and personal improvement, is thus a central theme of the *Republic*. Plato's conviction was also borne out in his own life, as it is believed that, following his association with Socrates, he burnt the poetry he had written in earlier years.

If philosophical study is, for Plato, the route to knowledge and virtue, and the optimal preparation for government, this is certainly contingent on the *kind* of philosophy that is practised. Much of what passed for philosophy in Athens, according to Books VI and VII, was really unworthy of the name, and its exponents were charlatans and fools. There is little doubt that Plato's principal targets were the Sophists, whose cleverness in banter and wordplay was, in his eyes, a poor shadow of the true philosopher's quest for truth through conceptual analysis, and whose demand for payment contrasted starkly with Socrates' engagement in the subject for the sake of knowledge alone. In condemning the way philosophical thought was undertaken by many in his society, Plato again plays the role of social critic, whilst simultaneously setting apart his own teacher and defending him against those, notably the playwright Aristophanes, who claimed that he too was engaged in sophistry.[1]

2.3. PSYCHOLOGY AND EPISTEMOLOGY

Among the topics receiving extended treatment in the *Republic* are the structure of the human soul and the nature of knowledge. In *Republic* IV, Plato proposes the distinctive view that the soul consists of three different parts or faculties, whose power and significance varies depending on the character of the individual concerned. These parts are distinguished primarily by the types of ends whose pursuit each of them motivates. First, there is the rational part, which is predominant in the just person's soul, and encompasses the motivation to seek what one believes is good, together with a more specific love of knowledge and learning. The 'spirited' part of us, distinct from the rational, causes us to seek such self-aggrandizing goals as honour, status, victory in war, and revenge against our enemies. Finally, the appetitive or desiring element comprises a range of motivations for baser ends, from material wealth, through various kinds of pleasure and distraction, to sexual gratification. In Book VIII, Plato suggests that some of these appetites are 'better', i.e. more orderly, than others: desires for financial security, for instance, are among the less degenerate, whereas sadistic or incestuous sexual desires feature as the very worst.

The *Republic* constructs an extended analogy between the various classes of citizen within the state and the different faculties of the soul. The intensively educated guardians, whose role is to govern the city, Plato likens to reason; the city's soldiers he deems parallel to spirit; and the different kinds of productive workers he links with the various appetites. This analogy is used in Book IV to illustrate important similarities between the virtues associated with states, and souls, respectively. It is also employed in Books VIII and IX to sketch the various corrupt types of city and of human character.

The topic of knowledge is addressed in the central section of the *Republic*: Books V to VII. Plato's epistemological views are again radical, as he argues in direct opposition to much commonsense opinion that the only field in which knowledge can be attained is in the investigation of abstract concepts such as goodness, justice, wisdom and others susceptible to philosophical analysis. By contrast, we cannot know anything of the physical realm we perceive through our senses, and therefore those who devote their attention to this sphere – so-called 'lovers of sights and sounds' (476b) – can never truly acquire knowledge through their studies, but only belief or opinion.

Plato's epistemology is closely linked to his metaphysics, the most idiosyncratic feature of which is the assertion of the existence of *Forms*. These are abstract objects which possess properties in unconditional, unalloyed ways. The Form of Good, for example, is an unconditionally good object – as Plato might otherwise say, 'goodness itself' – and the same applies to the Forms of other properties: justice, largeness, redness, and so on. Forms are not accessible to the senses but rather to the intellect, and it is their nature, on Plato's account, which philosophical investigations seek to clarify. Thus, by philosophically analysing a property such as goodness, one may come to know, in Plato's terms, the character of the Form that possesses this property unconditionally. Such knowledge is therefore the province of philosophers, and since Forms are for Plato the *only* truly knowable objects, those who do not philosophize lack knowledge altogether (though most of them are blissfully unaware of the fact).

Plato's account of knowledge and its possession is attractively illustrated in Book VII by the famous metaphor of the Cave. The bulk of human beings are like prisoners who live their entire lives tied down in an underground chamber, watching the shadows reflected on a wall by objects carried behind their heads. These people may pronounce confidently on what they see; they believe, then, that they have knowledge of the world they inhabit. In fact, however, they are perpetually deceived, not realizing that the shadows they see are mere images, let alone apprehending the existence of a world outside the cave. Only a few – those who engage in philosophical study – are able to break their bonds, leave the cave and learn the true nature of reality; in the metaphor, the outside world corresponds to the realm of Forms, of which the majority are ignorant. However, should those who have seen this realm return to the cave and try to inform the bound prisoners about it, they are highly unlikely to be believed. This corresponds to the masses being unwilling to accept philosophers' superior knowledge, choosing instead to trust their own, cave-bound prejudices.

Plato's epistemology is highly relevant to his political philosophy, since it is largely because philosophers have knowledge, and others do not, that the former are deemed more suitable to govern the state. Philosophers' understanding of Forms such as those of goodness and virtue – that is, the nature of goodness and virtue themselves – enables them to design policies to render the state, and its citizens' lives, as good and virtuous as possible. Existing societies' reluctance to embrace philosophical rule, moreover, ties in with the refusal of the ignorant cave-dwellers to accept that theoreticians have the knowledge they themselves are lacking.

The next section, constituting the core of this commentary, contains more in-depth accounts of the *Republic*'s arguments, together with a range of critical analysis, exposition of ideas in important secondary literature, and discussion questions – many of which encourage readers to assess the relevance of Plato's views to current issues and debates. While sections of the original text will be treated in broadly sequential order, the commentary will be divided in terms of the themes which dominate different passages of the work, in some cases overlapping between consecutive books. In order to gain clearer comprehension of Plato's overall views, there will be some cross-references in the commentary to passages of the *Republic* before or after those presently under consideration. The English versions of quotations used are taken from Reeve's revision of Grube's translation, as detailed in section 5.1. References use the traditional *Stephanus* page and section numbers, as printed in the margins of most editions.

CHAPTER 3

READING THE TEXT

3.1. BOOK I – A TANGLED WEB

It was noted in section 1.2 how the form of Book I differs from that of the remainder of the *Republic*. The content of the discussion concerns justice, and the dialogue divides broadly into two sections: first, Socrates' debates with Cephalus and his son Polemachus (329c–336); and secondly, a somewhat heated argument between Socrates and Thrasymachus (336b onwards). These two parts of the dialogue pit Socrates against two sharply differing approaches to the subject of justice, each of which he ultimately rejects, but both of which reflect important ethical positions to which Plato succeeds in drawing his readers' attention.

The arguments in Book I are numerous, often quite technical, and densely packed, so that it requires considerable care to keep a clear view of what proposition is being attacked or defended in any given passage. It has also been widely argued that many, if not most, of Socrates' arguments in this book are distinctly unconvincing, and depend precisely on the sort of linguistic sophistry that he condemns – in other passages of the *Republic*. Indeed, we find that by the end of the first book Socrates himself seems unsatisfied with his own conclusions. It is important, then, that readers consider what exactly Plato's own attitude is to the claims presented here. Does he intend us to agree with Socrates on every point, and if not, what message should we take from this discussion?

Before addressing these points, I shall set out and evaluate the main arguments in Book I. Due to space constraints, and the density of the text, what follows has the character of a rather schematic survey, seeking to identify the main points of interest, while also indicating the issues that will receive more detailed treatment later in the *Republic*.

3.1.1. Debates with Cephalus and Polemachus

The question of the nature of justice first arises as follows. Socrates is described as meeting his friend Polemachus on the way back from a religious festival, whereupon they go to call on Polemachus' father, Cephalus, an old, wealthy man with an interest, albeit rather superficial, in philosophical debate. Socrates asks Cephalus what he sees as the main benefit of his riches, and Cephalus replies that because he is rich, he has no reason to engage in unjust acts, such as cheating or deception, or failing to pay his debts to other people or (in sacrifices) to the gods (331b).

In response, Socrates questions Cephalus' understanding of the term 'justice'; specifically, he wonders what conception of justice is implied by the set of supposedly unjust acts the old man has identified. It seems, on Cephalus' account, that being just involves telling the truth and paying one's debts. Socrates, however, argues against this view: if you have borrowed weapons from a friend and the friend goes criminally insane, it does not seem just to repay your debt by returning the weapons (331c). Equally, he says it is not necessarily just to tell the truth to a madman (to coin an example, if you know your daughter is being pursued by an axe-murderer, and this man comes to your door and asks you her whereabouts, it would not be just to give him the facts of the case). Such examples seem to show that justice need not involve an absolute commitment to debt-repayment or truth-telling.

Cephalus is unwilling to engage in any further discussion, and exits with a convenient excuse. The argument, however, is immediately continued by his son Polemachus (331e). Polemachus adapts his father's suggestion that justice involves repaying debts, suggesting rather that it entails giving people what is owed to them, in the broader sense of giving them their due, or treating them appropriately (332b). He further specifies this to mean that a just person does good to his friends and harm to his enemies. For interpretative purposes, one might separate Polemachus' two points here, although in the text they are somewhat conflated. The general thesis – **P1 (332a)**: Justice is treating people appropriately (giving them their due) – does not necessarily imply the more specific claim **P2 (332a–b)**: Justice is doing good to friends and harm to enemies.

Plato's subsequent dialogue does not address P1 directly, as Socrates immediately sets out to attack P2. It will, however, be worthwhile, in surveying his arguments, to note which if any of them also tells against P1. Taken on its own, P1 seems a plausible, albeit somewhat vague, proposition; the idea of a just distribution of goods, for example, is often characterized in terms of giving people *appropriate* amounts. It is also notable that P1 effectively diffuses the axe-murderer problem mentioned above: since it is not appropriate to tell the truth to someone who will use the information to commit murder, such actions are ruled out by a commitment to justice as defined by P1, making this definition coherent with common intuition about such cases.

Socrates uses four arguments against the more questionable P2, which span the section (332c–336). I shall summarize and comment on each.

a. (332c–333e). Socrates begins by treating justice as a kind of craft or skill (*technē*). Most crafts, he claims, operate in a specific field; for instance, the craft of medicine operates in the field of pre-scribing drugs and diet, cookery in providing flavour to food, and so forth. According to P2, it seems the field in which the craft of justice operates is that of doing good to friends and harm to enemies. But the ability to do friends good and enemies harm, Socrates claims, requires, in any given situation, some craft other than justice. In a medical context, it is a doctor's craft which enables one to cure one's friends or poison one's enemies; in seafaring, navigational ability best equips one to ensure a friend a safe passage, or dash an enemy upon the rocks. But, according to Socrates, there is no particular field of expertise where justice (abstracted from any other craft) best enables one to do harm or good.

b. (333e–334b). The second argument follows immediately upon the first, and centres on the claim that the craft (*technē*) enabling the achievement of any given end generally coexists with the ability to achieve its opposite. For example, a doctor's skill in preventing illness also implies that he knows how to induce it; and a good guard is also a good thief because of his knowledge of security procedures. So, similarly, if the just person's skill is in protecting his friends' finances (using Socrates' example), it follows that he will also be adept at swindling friends, should he decide to do so. Generalizing from this point, Socrates argues that if justice is defined as skill in benefiting friends and harming enemies, such a skill would coexist with the capacity to do the opposites: good to enemies or harm to friends. But it would surely be wrong to characterize justice in this way; hence P2 is inadequate.

Neither of these arguments is very convincing, the problem with both being that they assume that justice is a craft or skill in the same way as medicine, navigation or guardianship, despite the fact that nothing in P2 (or P1 for that matter) implies that this is so.[1] Surely the important difference between justice and these crafts is that while the latter are practices which enable agents to achieve certain ends (such as curing disease, or safeguarding property) *should they choose to do so*, justice is a disposition actually *to choose* certain ends rather than others. Thus, it seems wrong to interpret P2 to mean that just people are those most *able* to do their friends good and enemies harm, as Socrates' objections imply. A more generous, and plausible, reading of Polemachus' thesis is that these are the types of actions just people typically choose to perform.

Insofar, then, as Socrates' first two arguments interpret Polemachus' proposals in a misleading fashion, the arguments themselves are unpersuasive. This said, an important point has emerged from this passage, namely that it is wrong to think of justice as being a type of skill; rather, it is a disposition to choose particular ends. There is admittedly a further question of whether being just sometimes *also* requires some measure of skill – after all, it is arguably not sufficient for justice that one *aims* to treat people appropriately (say), and it may also be necessary that one knows what is appropriate and how to allocate it. A judge who makes every effort to be fair and scrupulous towards those in his court, but who is inept at decision-making and therefore makes wildly inappropriate verdicts, may not be considered a just judge despite his honourable intentions. If the label 'just' is not applicable, that implies that some skill – namely judicial skill – is a necessary condition for justice in this context. The intention to make fair decisions is necessary too, but it is (arguably) not enough on its own.

Returning to the text, Socrates next argument against P2 is as follows: **c. (334c–335b)**. It is possible that someone who seeks to do good to his friends and harm to his enemies may, perhaps unintentionally, choose good people as enemies or bad ones as friends. If this happens, and P2 is true, it follows that justice sometimes involves doing harm to good agents and benefiting bad ones, which seems implausible.

This argument is straightforward, and a convincing objection to P2 as stated. Indeed, Polemachus responds by adapting his position to **P3 (335a)**: Justice is doing good to people who are good (and whom one believes are good) and doing harm to those who are bad (and whom one believes are bad). This account raises several questions, not all of which Plato considers. For instance, P3 offers no prescription for how we should treat those whom we think are good, but are in fact bad, or vice versa. Perhaps more significantly, it says nothing about the treatment of those about whose moral status we have *no* beliefs – strangers for example – whereas it would seem natural to think that justice requires treating these people in certain ways. Such objections are relatively trivial, however, compared with Socrates' next claim, namely:

d. (335b–336). A just person would not harm anyone at all. This contention resonates with what we might term a 'pacifist' view of justice. The argument which Socrates uses to substantiate it, however, is rather tortuous. Harming something, he says, entails making it worse, and making it worse involves removing from it the particular quality that makes it good. In the case of a human being, the quality that makes one good is justice. Hence, harming a human being involves making him or her less just. But justice surely cannot involve making people less just. Hence, justice cannot involve harming anyone.

Whether or not one agrees with the conclusion, this argument is highly dubious. There is, firstly, no obvious reason to accept the premise that harming someone entails making them 'less good'.[2] It may rather involve simply making them less well off, perhaps in terms of health, freedom, or general quality of life, and it might indeed be argued that justice *does*, on occasion, require denying these goods to individuals (this, for example, is a necessary feature of just punishment). One might also doubt Socrates' assumption that making someone worse involves making them less just, which, as Annas notes,[3] appears in the text as an unargued assertion. Socrates' method of arguing for his 'pacifist' claim is, then, barely persuasive. Polemachus, however, is persuaded by it, and consequently abandons his attempt to define justice, at which point a new character, Thrasymachus, interrupts the discussion and steers it onto a different course.

What can we take from the exchange between Polemachus and Socrates? The latter's arguments are, for the most part, unsatisfying, though he does suggest some possible grounds upon which P2 and P3 might be opposed. He does little, however, to undermine the more general thesis P1, that justice involves treating people appropriately, a view which emerges largely unscathed, despite its vagueness and generality (it can offer few prescriptions for action unless the term 'appropriate' is more clearly specified). As regards the more general message of this section, we might, following Annas,[4] interpret Plato as targeting a certain approach to the definition of justice, common in both his and our own cultures, which understands the concept in terms of following certain rules of conduct. For Cephalus, being just is telling the truth and paying debts; for Polemachus, it is doing good to friends and harm to enemies. Several of Socrates' points demonstrate a problem with such lists of rules; namely, that for any proposed 'rule of just conduct' it is possible to find circumstances where, intuitively, it is not just to obey this rule. It is, for example, not just to pay one's debts if this involves returning weapons to a madman, nor to aid one's friends if they turn out to be villains. Generalizing from these cases, rigid adherence to a set of rules is unlikely to deliver just behaviour in all circumstances. What may be required is a more flexible capacity to determine what to do in different situations as they arise.

Another difficulty with the Cephalus-Polemachus approach, which will become clearer as the *Republic* progresses, is that to define justice in terms of how someone acts assigns no weight to the psychology underlying their actions. If justice is simply adherence to given rules of conduct, then someone who obeys such rules simply because he thinks it will benefit him to do so, or fears the consequences of doing otherwise, will qualify as just. It could be countered, however, that justice requires not only the performance of certain acts but also the presence of certain motives for action, such as a desire to see fairness prevail.

3.1.2. Thrasymachus: his character and arguments

Before examining Thrasymachus' arguments and Socrates' responses to them, it is worth considering the contrast between the former's characterization and those of Cephalus and Polemachus in earlier discussions. Thrasymachus is given an extremely rude and aggressive persona, manifest in numerous ways. When he joins the dialogue, he is said to 'hurl himself' at Polemachus and Socrates (336b), and accuse them of stupidity (336c). He then insults Socrates several times, at one stage referring to his 'snotty nose' (343a). He asks for money in return for philosophical instruction, a practice associated with the Sophists whom Plato so despised (337d). And from (350), he becomes sullen and refuses to engage with Socrates' arguments, feigning agreement with him merely as a form of sarcasm.

This highly unsympathetic (albeit entertaining) portrayal of Thrasymachus is significant when we consider the kind of philosophical position he represents. He is, to borrow Annas' term,[5] an immoralist – a positive advocate of an unjust life, which he believes to be in an agent's best interests. Socrates' previous protagonists, Cephalus and Polemachus, by contrast, had represented relatively conventional viewpoints on morality – broadly sympathetic to justice, but conceiving it in terms of certain rules of action. These individuals, moreover, were correspondingly portrayed as upright, decent types, who conversed politely with Socrates but who were unable to respond adequately to his arguments. If we interpret Plato's characterizations as revealing his attitudes to the respective theories expounded, we might say he seems to regard conventional morality as worthy and respectable, but as lacking answers to carefully framed philosophical objections. Immoralism, or scepticism about morality, is by contrast associated with aggression, petulance and greed.

Socrates is again presented as 'winning' the argument with Thrasymachus, at least insofar as the latter gives up contradicting him. However, we shall see that the arguments Socrates uses against the immoralist are mostly tortuous and unconvincing, as even Plato himself seems aware by the end. There is no clear cut case in Book I, then, for why immoralism is wrong. Before we can draw any general conclusions about the message of this section, however, we need to examine its arguments.

Thrasymachus begins by offering a view that justice is 'the advantage of the stronger' (338c); by 'the stronger', he apparently means the ruler of a political state (338d). His opening gambit, then, is **T1 (339a)**: Justice is what is in the advantage of an established political ruler. To be just, it follows, is to do what is in the interests of the ruler(s) of your society. Socrates immediately attacks this claim as follows (339b–e). Justice, as Thrasymachus believes, involves obeying the laws and orders laid down by your rulers. But there are some cases, says Socrates, where rulers, perhaps mistakenly, issue laws whose obedience is not to their own advantage. In this situation, justice cannot both involve obeying rulers and advantaging them, as it is impossible to do both simultaneously.

Thrasymachus' response is that the conflict identified by Socrates cannot occur, since all rulers essentially make laws and give orders in their own interest, and anyone who does not do so cannot be counted as a genuine ruler (340d–341). He substantiates this by arguing that ruling is a craft (*technē*) whose purpose is to benefit the ruler's own interests – someone who does not benefit himself is thus failing to rule properly. Socrates disputes this, arguing that just as success in the crafts of medicine and navigation are not primarily beneficial to the practitioner but to some other agent (the patient or passenger), so skilful ruling is not beneficial to the ruler himself but to his subjects (342a–e). But Thrasymachus replies, with considerable invective, that the exercise of any craft is typically in the craftsman's interest, giving examples of shepherds and cowherds who raise animals in order to profit from their sale. Likewise, he insists, a skilled ruler benefits his people only insofar as this furthers his own advantage too (343a–344c). Socrates once more denies this, claiming that the 'true shepherd' promotes his flock's welfare for non-selfish reasons, and citing the fact that politicians demand payment for their work as evidence that ruling is not intrinsically advantageous to them (345b–347e).

This discussion on the nature and function of government strays some way from the original task of defining justice, though it is relevant to issues about the ideal political system subsequently raised in the *Republic*. Socrates, however, switches the argument (347e) to a matter of 'far more importance' in Thrasymachus' long speech (343b–344c), namely his claim that: **T2 (343d)**: Just people are always worse off than unjust ones. It follows from this that anyone who wishes successfully to promote his own self-interest should be as unjust as possible. Thrasymachus exemplifies this in several ways: unjust people, he says, do better in financial partnerships than just ones because they are willing to cheat their partners, and play the public tax and benefit system to their advantage while the just suffer from their commitment to obeying rules (343d). Here, then, is Thrasymachus' immoralism – the view, in a nutshell, that immorality pays.

There is a point of criticism, not explicitly raised in the text but identified by recent commentators, concerning the relationship between Thrasymachus' claims, T1 and T2. On the one hand, the view that justice involves benefiting rulers (T1) ties in with the above example of taxation: just people pay taxes to those in government, advantaging the rulers (T1) but making themselves financially worse off (T2). On the other hand, as Cross and Woozley note,[6] T1 and T2 seem inconsistent when we consider the activities of rulers themselves. If justice always benefits rulers, it follows that a ruler, when just, advantages himself. But this claim flatly contradicts T2, which states that being just always entails one's own *dis*advantage.

There are various ways of responding to this apparent inconsistency. One could suggest that Plato is deliberately presenting Thrasymachus as a muddled thinker in order to denigrate the philosophical views ascribed to him. Another route, favoured by Annas,[7] is to say that when advocating T1, Thrasymachus is specifically considering what it means for an ordinary private citizen to be just; namely, to obey the rulers of his state (who are assumed to be self-serving) thus benefiting them rather than himself. For a ruler, however, justice involves promoting the interests of one's subjects at one's own expense, as Thrasymachus implies (344e). In both instances, then, justice entails benefiting others and disadvantaging oneself, a view consonant with T2.

3.1.3. Socrates' first defence of justice

In the final passages of Book I, Socrates levels a series of objections at the claim that unjust people are better off than the just. I shall pass over the first of these, a pedantic and somewhat flimsy argument likening the unjust person to an ignoramus (348b–350c),[8] and examine what are his three most interesting points, before considering what overall conclusions can be drawn from this section.

a. (351a–352d). Socrates argues that, contrary to T2, unjust people may be worse off than just ones, because they cannot achieve goals requiring cooperation with others. He uses the example of a band of thieves (351c), who share the common unjust purpose of carrying out a robbery. Unless they behave trustworthily towards each other, thus demonstrating some form of just behaviour, their joint goal cannot be attained. More generally, insofar as injustice essentially produces hatred and infighting among its adherents, unjust people cannot acquire the benefits that stem from forming and maintaining alliances.

This is an interesting argument, more cogent than many in Book I. However, there are points that an opponent might make in response. First, he might say there are ways of holding together alliances which do not involve a mutual commitment to justice. If, for instance, every member of Socrates' gang of thieves profited from being part of the gang, each might cooperate with the others simply to further his own interests.[9] His motives need not involve any altruistic feeling, or indeed any desire to be just or honourable.

Socrates might counter that insofar as such cooperation is based solely on the wish to profit individually from a joint venture, it is likely to be short-term. As soon as the spoils of the thieves' alliance are secured, it is in the interest of each, *qua* unjust agent, to cheat the others of their shares. Hence, it may not be possible for *all* those involved in the conspiracy to profit, as some will eventually triumph over others. Thrasymachus could reply, however, that the most cunning and resourceful of them profit immensely – thus, as he argues, 'injustice, *if it is on a large enough scale*, is stronger, freer, and more masterly than justice' (344c, my italics). In other words, the most accomplished villains fare better than any just individuals do. This is admittedly weaker than his original view (T2) that unjust people are *always* better off than just ones, but it still makes certain (successful) unjust agents the happiest people of all.

b. (352a). In the middle of his argument for S6, Socrates mentions the following, distinct, claim. In the same way as groups of unjust people suffer from division and conflict, so an individual unjust agent undergoes an internal psychological civil war; rather than being of one mind, he is 'an enemy to himself' (ibid.).

This is another interesting view, which takes on considerable importance later in the *Republic*. At this stage, however, it is unclear how exactly Socrates conceives of the unjust man's internal conflicts. On the one hand, we might well think of certain unjust people being riven by guilt, or hating themselves for their evil deeds. But surely, an opponent might claim, this does not apply to all unjust individuals: some may be perfectly happy satisfying their selfish desires at the expense of others, and feel no scruples about doing so. More argument, then, is needed to show why internal conflict necessarily accompanies injustice. As we shall see in Book IV, when Plato spells out his detailed theory of human psychology, he will claim that the human soul has parts which, in cases of injustice, are essentially disordered. But the point about internal division, as stated in Book I, is too undeveloped to be persuasive.[10]

c. (352d–354a). Socrates' final argument in Book I differs from those preceding it insofar as it does not only seek to establish the disadvantages of injustice, but seeks positively to show that a just life is a flourishing and happy one (a life of *eudaimonia*). It begins with the premise that the function (*ergon*) of an object is something that only it can do, or something that it does better than anything else; for example, the function of eyes is seeing, and the function of a pruning knife is cutting vines. In order to perform its function well, an object needs a particular virtue (*aretē*): keen vision in the case of eyes, sharpness (presumably) in that of a knife. If, however, an object has the corresponding defect (blindness, or bluntness), it will perform its function badly. Now, the functions of a human soul are, Socrates claims, to manage, rule, deliberate, and above all to *live*. And the virtue associated with a human soul is justice, with injustice the associated deficiency. But since, according to Socrates, an object fulfils its function well by exhibiting its associated virtue, it is the just soul which performs a soul's specific function – that is, lives – well, whilst the unjust one lives badly. Moreover, since anyone who lives well is happy and flourishing (*eudaimōn*), this is true of the just person but not the unjust.

There are various ways of objecting to this argument, one of which is to reject the view that a soul has a function in the same way as eyes and knives. But Socrates has defined an object's function specifically as the activity characteristically associated with a thing of its kind, and it is plausible to assert that the characteristic activity of a human soul is to live a (human) life. There is still a serious problem with the argument, however, which is identified by Annas;[11] and concerns the premise that the virtue, which best promotes a successful human life, is that of justice. It is not clear how Socrates thinks this has been established, and it is wide open to Thrasymachus to claim that, on the contrary, it is the unjust who flourish best in human society. In defending his premise, perhaps Socrates could appeal to his previous arguments, for example that the unjust man cannot attain goods requiring cooperation, and that his soul is divided. But, as we have seen, these points are not fully substantiated in Book I, and it is not clear that they offer a strong enough basis to assert that justice, rather than injustice, aids successful living. But unless this premise is established, the final argument also fails.

The package of arguments that Socrates has used to show that a just life is 'better', in various respects, than an unjust one, will probably not convince most readers, though it does gesture towards some points which Plato will develop later on. From an interpretative viewpoint, moreover, it is worth noting Thrasymachus' response to this Socratic barrage of points. While ostensibly giving up the argumentative struggle, and outwardly agreeing with all of Socrates' points, he makes it perfectly clear that he is by no means genuinely persuaded. He asserts, for instance, that while he could answer Socrates back, he chooses rather to 'give assent' as one would to an 'old wife's tale' (350d–e), later explaining such reticence on grounds that he does not wish to offend Socrates' supporters who are gathered around (352b). Maybe his refusal to argue could be taken as evidence that he has no case to plead. But, in the light of other factors, one might rather interpret his continued scepticism as indicating doubt on Plato's own part about the legitimacy of the arguments he expresses through Socrates' mouth. At the very least, it suggests that such arguments are considered insufficient to convince someone of Thrasymachus' immoralist mindset that he would be better off converting to a just lifestyle.[12]

What factors, then, support this latter interpretation? First, there is Socrates' own comment at the end of Book I (354b), where he says that it is really impossible to know whether or not the just life is happy until one has defined precisely what justice is – a definition he himself has not yet established. Secondly, if we look ahead to the beginning of Book II, we see that others, besides Thrasymachus, are unsatisfied by Socrates' case. Glaucon, who is instinctively sympathetic to Socrates, asks whether he really wants to persuade his listeners that it is better for them to be just than unjust, commenting that if he does, he has certainly not succeeded thus far. Again, the message might be that whatever the merits of the arguments outlined in Book I, they are not enough to convince someone who does not already accept Socrates' view of justice. Hence, much of what follows in the *Republic* is Plato's attempt to supply a much more detailed and discursive style of argument to achieve this end.

Discussion questions:
(a) What are the strengths and weaknesses of the dialogue form as a means of expressing philosophical ideas and arguments?
(b) Is the search for a single correct definition of justice a viable or

worthwhile project, or should we simply admit that the term may be used with different meanings in different contexts?

3.2. THE CHALLENGE TO SOCRATES (357a–369b)

Book II begins by focusing the debate firmly on the question of whether and how it is in an individual's interest to be just. Glaucon and Adeimantus, two brothers, pick up the claim which Socrates has just defended rather weakly, namely that it is better for an agent's self-interest to live justly rather than unjustly. This view, the brothers argue, is contrary to the opinions held by the vast majority, who believe that it is advantageous to be unjust provided one escapes undetected, and moreover that any benefits of the just life are merely incidental products of social (and possibly divine) systems of reward and retribution.

The form of the brothers' challenge is straightforward. Each expounds what they consider commonly held views about the relative unhappiness of the just life, and asks Socrates to show, by philosophical argument, how and why such views are incorrect. Unlike Thrasymachus in Book I, Glaucon and Adeimantus have sympathy for the notion that justice is a worthwhile goal; indeed, Adeimantus explicitly says that he 'wants to hear' that the opposite of Thrasymachus' immoralist position is true (367a). Both brothers are doubtful, though, whether there is really a good reason to think that the just prosper while the unjust live in misery; sober reflections on the realities of life suggest this is wishful thinking. If, therefore, Socrates genuinely wants to change popular opinion, he needs a very strong argument to disprove what many purport to know from first-hand experience.

3.2.1. Why be just?

Glaucon's speech begins (357b) with a threefold division between different categories of goods. First, there are things that are desired for themselves, rather than for their consequences; these include 'harmless pleasures' that we enjoy for their own sakes, rather than any longer term benefit – perhaps things like parties, and eating chocolate. Secondly, there are things we *both* desire for their own sake *and* for what comes from them; Glaucon gives the examples of knowledge, sight, and health. It is considered intrinsically valuable to be knowledgeable, and many pursue education for this reason alone, but knowledge might also help, for instance, when it comes to pursuing a career. The third and final category of good includes things that are *only* valuable for their consequences and *not* in themselves. Examples here are said to include physical training and medicine. Drinking cough mixture may be unpleasant in itself, but we appreciate the relief it brings in due course.

When Socrates claims (357e–358a) that he would place justice into the second category – something good both in itself and for its consequences – Glaucon counters that this is not what most people would say. They would rather group justice with medicine, as something practiced not for its intrinsic enjoyment (since being just in itself is somewhat burdensome), but rather for its consequential benefits, in particular the 'rewards and popularity that come from a *reputation* for justice' (358a, my italics).

It is worth noting that, throughout this talk of the goodness or desirability of justice, Plato seems concerned exclusively with goodness from the perspective of the just agent. The question Glaucon raises is, effectively, 'how does justice benefit *me*?', which can be answered by saying either that it is intrinsically beneficial, or that it has good consequences, or both. A critic might argue, however, that by framing the debate in these terms, Glaucon has already done some of the moral sceptic's work for him. When a character like Thrasymachus asks what reason he has to be just, he is effectively questioning how being just might contribute to his self-interest, thus enabling him to answer: 'not at all'. But now Glaucon, too, has chosen to measure the goodness of a just life solely from the perspective of the person living it. Many people might claim, however, that it is good to be just, not because *you* necessarily benefit, but for some reason unrelated to your own self-interest. The reason for being just might, for example, be to promote the welfare of others, or to do God's will, or to fulfil one's duty as enshrined in a moral law; none of which need refer directly to personal advantage of the just agent himself.

Of course, it is possible that Glaucon (and Plato) recognized this, but simply chose to address the more specific question of what *self-interested* reason there is for pursuing justice. And this question is surely important, not least because of its relevance in providing motivation for performing just acts – far more people would be likely to engage in them, if some self-interested benefit were thereby acquired.

3.2.2. The need for a social contract

Glaucon's argument for his view, that the only advantages of justice for the just agent lie in its consequences, proceeds as follows (beginning 358e). It is commonly held that to do injustice to another is good for oneself, but that to suffer injustice is bad. It follows from this that the best scenario for an individual is to do injustice to others without suffering any in return, and that the worst is to suffer injustice whilst doing none in retaliation. However, Glaucon also argues that for someone who lacks the power to do injustice to others while avoiding its receipt, it is preferable neither to do nor to suffer from unjust acts, than both to engage in them and be their victim. Hence, most people's preferences regarding their own and others' justice are as follows:

Preference	Self	Others
First	Unjust	Just
Second	Just	Just
Third	Unjust	Unjust
Fourth	Just	Unjust

Thus, the ideal situation is to live in a world where other people treat you well, but where you can exploit their good offices to unfair advantage. Next best is a society where everyone, yourself included, is cooperative and trustworthy. Worse than this is a 'dog-eat-dog' scenario, where you take your chances in a battle for survival among fellow villains. But even this is preferable to being the sole just agent in an otherwise corrupt world, where you suffer at others' hands and are too scrupulous to pay them back.

Now, if all or most people's preferences are ordered in this way, a serious problem arises, which modern game-theorists term the 'Prisoners' Dilemma'. Suppose that, with the above preference-ordering, you are asked to make the decision whether to be just or unjust. What are the consequences of either course? Well, first, suppose that others can be trusted to behave justly. If you act justly too, your second favourite scenario will result: a society of mutual cooperation. If, however, you choose to be unjust and take advantage of others' goodness, you will fare even better, since your first preference will be attained. What, then, if you believe that other people will be unjust? Again, if you yourself act unjustly, you get your third preference – 'dog eat dog'. If, on the other hand, you are just, the result is your least favourite scenario – 'dogs eat you'. It seems, then, that however others choose to behave, whether justly or unjustly, you will attain an outcome you rank more highly by being unjust than by being just. Moreover – and here is the crux – if everyone in society shares the same preference-ordering and goes through the reasoning process outlined, everyone will reach the same conclusion, that their best strategy is one of injustice. But if they act accordingly, the overall result is the world that each one of them individually ranks only third best: the world where everyone is unjust. The consequence, then, of each individual trying to maximize their own preference satisfaction is a scenario where no one is particularly well-off.

Glaucon's speech does not actually contain the full argument for the Prisoner's Dilemma as set out here. It does, however, analyse the preference-ordering among human beings that gives rise to the problem, and also suggests a well-known solution to it, namely that everyone makes a contractual agreement with each other 'neither to do injustice nor to suffer it' (359a). In actual societies, this is manifest in a set of 'laws and covenants which prescribe just behaviour' (ibid.), supported by a system of rewards and punishments. Through universal adherence to such a code, everyone can rest assured that they will not be the victim of others' injustice. The result, on the above analysis, is that everyone enjoys their second most favoured situation, one of universal justice, rather than their third. There is a danger that people will attempt to cheat on the contract, tempted by the prospect of first-preference satisfaction, by taking advantage of others' lawfulness, but this must be stamped out by the law, for if universally followed it would again result in the third-best society. Glaucon thus speaks of 'nature [being] forced by law into the perversion of treating fairness with respect' (359c); the implication being that, left to our own individual devices, we are naturally disposed to injustice, and so we need a collectively constructed artifice, in the form of the legal system, to bring about just conduct.

3.2.3. Being just versus appearing just

Even if social sanctions exist to promote universal just conduct, it remains possible for some powerful individuals to avoid them, in which case there is no reason, in terms of self-interest, for these people to pay justice any regard. This difficulty is illustrated by Glaucon with the story of Gyges' ring (359c–360d). The story tells of a shepherd who finds a ring which gives him the power of invisibility, which he uses to fulfil his desires for fame and fortune: he seduces the queen, kills the king and takes over the kingdom. The magic ring means that Gyges' unjust deeds cannot be detected, so he is effectively immune from any kind of punishment. Glaucon's point is that anyone who acquires the power to do as they wish with impunity will surely use it to increase their wealth, status, power and sexual gratification, harming enemies and aiding friends as they see fit. Presented with the opportunity to be unjust and get away with it, then, virtually no one would find value in just action. The only reason most of us *are* just is that we do not have Gyges' degree of power; given our limitations, we best serve ourselves through justice, because we thereby attain the rewards and avoid the punishments socially instituted to encourage such behaviour. This supports Glaucon's initial claim that being just is desirable for its consequences – the benefits of being considered law-abiding, and the avoidance of punishment. In itself, however, it does nothing whatsoever for an individual's interests.

Glaucon's final and most memorable point (beginning 360e) builds on the above as follows. He contrasts the fortunes of two individuals: one who is completely wicked but manages to maintain a reputation for justice, and one who is just, but who is generally regarded as villainous. Glaucon argues that the first individual enjoys the vastly preferable life: he is praised and fêted by society as a model citizen, whilst using his concealed injustice to exploit others and thus acquire additional profits. On the other hand, the agent who is just but believed to be the opposite will suffer all the chastisements imposed on the worst offenders in society, including the rack, chains, blinding and impalement (361e). Given the comparison between these two lives, Glaucon contends, it is not justice itself that is beneficial to an individual, but rather the *appearance* of justice. Hence, in order to have the best life possible, one should cultivate a reputation for justice in others' eyes, whilst secretly pursuing injustice to further one's own advantage.

3.2.4. Adeimantus' speech and Socrates' task

After Glaucon ends by challenging Socrates to show where his arguments have gone astray, and why the just life is intrinsically desirable after all, Adeimantus interjects (362d) with a more rhetorical speech than Glaucon's, peppered with references to contemporary mythology and literature. In terms of content, the brothers' speeches cover largely similar ground, though Adeimantus adds one substantive point concerning the respective status of just and unjust individuals in the opinions of the gods. While, as Glaucon suggests, one might be able to deceive other human beings that one is just when one is not, it seems less plausible that gods could be kept in the dark – an omniscient being, after all, necessarily knows the truth about one's conduct. If, then, as is widely believed, the gods reward justice and punish injustice (see 363b–e for Athenian accounts of how), perhaps the promise of divine sanctions could constitute a reason for actually being just, rather than merely appearing so to one's fellow human beings?

Adeimantus argues, however, that it does not, for the simple reason that the gods can be 'bought off' exacting punishments on those who can offer them sufficient payment (364c). This means that the unjust person with the worldly reputation for justice is in the strongest position to purchase such clemency, as his conduct acquires him a large store of ill-gotten gains to spend on the necessary gifts and sacrifices. He does concede it possible that the gods do not exist, or that they are not concerned with human affairs (365d–e), in which case divine considerations have no impact on whether one has reason to be just. But if the gods *are* there and do intervene, then according to Greek laws and mythology, they are essentially biddable, and thus of no danger to the economically successful unjust agent.

It is, of course, open to an opponent to deny that existing deities are corruptible in this way; indeed, Socrates himself later dismisses the view that gods can be paid off with sacrifices (390e), on grounds that an unearthly being could have no interest in earthly possessions. If gods were thus immune to bribery, and treated people strictly according to their ethical status, then this would constitute a strong instrumental reason for being just.

The brothers' speeches form the basis for the central theme of the *Republic*, Socrates' defence of the just way of life. There is a point of some confusion, however, over precisely what Socrates is being asked to do. At the outset of Glaucon's speech, he distinguishes between goods which are valued for themselves and those that are only valued for their consequences, suggesting that justice falls in the latter category. We might, then, take him to be asking Socrates why justice is intrinsically, rather than just consequentially, valuable. However, by the end of his contribution, Glaucon seems to have argued that it is not justice (i.e. *being* just) that has good consequences, but merely *seeming* to be just. This suggests that his question for Socrates is not whether justice is valuable for itself alone, but whether it – as opposed to its appearance – has *any* value for the just agent.

Similarly, when Adeimantus winds up his speech (367c–d), he appears to reiterate Glaucon's original challenge, asking that Socrates praise justice as something which, like sight, knowledge and health, is good not only for what comes from it (i.e. its consequences), but also for its own sake. But, again, immediately afterwards, he asks a slightly different question (367e), about the effects of justice and injustice on those who possess these qualities, as opposed to the effects of having just and unjust *reputations*. Here again, there is a running together of two separate issues: (a) whether and why justice is desirable for its own sake, or merely for its consequences; and (b) whether and why justice itself, rather than merely a reputation for justice, is desirable *per se*. Whilst this does appear a point of textual confusion, it is of course possible that Plato recognized the distinction between these questions and simply wished to consider both of them.

Discussion question:
Glaucon suggests that most people are only motivated to act justly because of a socially instituted system of rewards and punishments. Is this true, or what other sorts of motive might there be for just behaviour?

3.3. THE DEVELOPMENT OF THE CITY (368a–376c)

The section from the middle of Book II (368), when Socrates begins his response to Glaucon and Adeimantus, to the end of Book IV, where the discussion changes direction, contains much of the meat of the *Republic*. It is here that Plato develops, through Socrates' arguments, what appears to be his own, original account of the nature of justice, and begins to use this account to argue for the intrinsic desirability of the just life.

3.3.1. Socrates' approach to the argument

In order to assess the value of living justly, one must begin with a satisfactory definition of justice as a quality of an individual agent. Socrates argues, however, (368d–e) that to provide such a definition, we should first examine justice in a political context, by outlining the nature of a just city-state (*polis*). In a city, we find justice on a larger scale than in any single human being, and once we have seen the virtue of justice in this magnified form, we will be able to offer an account of the just individual person by analogy. The strategy Socrates will employ, therefore, is first to build a detailed model of a city; secondly, to analyse how the city achieves the virtue of justice; and thirdly, to apply what has been discovered to construct an analogous model of the just individual soul.

Socrates' proposed method of analysing justice is open to several criticisms. First, one might question whether the term 'justice' applied to a civic community need have anything like the same sense as it does when applied to a human being. As Cross and Woozley argue,[13] there are some words which have very different meanings when referring to these two objects. Take the term 'healthy'. The statement 'Socrates is healthy' is normally taken to mean that he is in good physical condition; 'Athens is healthy', by contrast, is most naturally interpreted as meaning that the city is conducive to the health of those who live there. With respect to justice, equally, there are reasons to doubt whether the term means the same when applied to a city as to an individual. It is often believed, for instance, that one aspect of justice in a state has to do with the way in which certain goods – wealth, opportunity, rights and so forth – are distributed among its citizens. There is no obvious analogy between this feature of political justice, and justice in an individual person. It would seem intuitively very odd to say that justice in an individual involves a distribution of goods between component parts.

Socrates' response to these objections might be first to point out that until he has offered his definition of justice, it is impossible to say whether or not it applies equally in both political and personal contexts. The proof of his approach lies in whether he can obtain a plausible account of individual justice through an analogy with justice in the city. As regards the point about political justice having a distributive element, moreover, we shall see that Socrates interprets this primarily in terms of a distribution of *power* between different classes of citizen, and that he does indeed postulate an equivalent distribution of power between the different faculties of a just person's soul. The details of this are addressed in sections 3.5 and 3.6 of this book.

3.3.2. The primitive city and justice

The search for an account of justice in a city begins at (369b), with an extended analysis of the reasons why human beings choose to organize into societies rather than managing on their own. The basis of the state is that none of us is self-sufficient. In order to fulfil our desires for food, shelter and clothing, groups of us 'gather in a single place to live together as partners and helpers. And such a settlement is called a city' (369b–c). To satisfy our needs most efficiently, we divide labour so that each person specializes in a particular task, producing a certain type of good (such as food or clothing) which he then supplies for his fellow citizens, in return for their providing him with the commodities in which *they* specialize.

This principle, which economists term 'division of labour', is justified in the *Republic* on two grounds. First, as Socrates points out, 'each of us differs somewhat in nature from the others' (370a–b). Muscular people, for example, may be naturally suited to manual labour, while the less able-bodied are better fitted for retailing. By assigning everyone a task appropriate to his natural constitution, efficiency in production is increased. The second reason for dividing labour (370b) is that, regardless of ability, someone will do a better job if he focuses on one craft or skill rather than having to combine several. Again, efficiency is reduced if a worker is distracted from performing one task by the need to perform various others.

There is a clear economic rationale, then, for forming communities where each person specializes in supplying a particular type of need. At (372a–d), we are given an overview of life in a city organized on such lines. There is simple food, shelter and clothing enough for all to live healthily, and everyone works hard at their craft but enjoys some relaxation and the company of their fellows. Despite the absence of luxury, this existence is depicted as a fairly attractive one. There is, moreover, a sense of Plato's harking back to a bucolic past era of peace, good health and rustic pleasures, a 'golden age' before the social, cultural and technological developments Athens had undergone. Admittedly, Glaucon intervenes to say that the dietary arrangements in the society Socrates has outlined would be suitable for a 'city of pigs' (372c–d), implying that the state which aims only at basic need-fulfilment lacks the additional amenities which make life comfortable and pleasant. Socrates, in response, accepts that we would need other types of workers to provide luxury goods: hunters, artists, servants, tutors and beauticians, to name but some. But he still appears to favour the city without service industries of these kinds, saying that the 'true' and 'healthy' city is the more simplistic one, while the luxurious city suffers 'a fever' (372e).

Given this claim, we might perhaps wonder why Plato does not make more of the primitive city when setting out his account of political justice. For while he praises it as 'true' and 'healthy', he never describes it as containing *just* arrangements; moreover, his account of the just city involves imposing certain political arrangements on a community which includes the very luxury industries he appears to decry. The explanation for this may be partly that the simpler city is considered an unobtainable ideal. Human nature being what it is, the desire for luxuries over and above what is necessary for comfortable survival will inevitably arise and demand satisfaction. This said, there are at least some of the more 'civilized' pleasures which Plato clearly believes we can and should do without; for instance, his account of the just state has no place for much of the art and poetry enjoyed in contemporary Athens.

There are other reasons, however, to think that the 'city of pigs' fails to meet the requirements for justice. First, as there is no mention of any rulers or legal institutions within this city, we might suppose that there will be few, if any, sanctions by which to enforce honest dealings between purveyors of the various trades. Even if the satisfaction of needs is sufficiently commonplace that few are motivated to steal, there is still the potential for certain individuals to 'free-ride' by enjoying more than their share of leisure-time whilst taking advantage of the goods produced by their fellows. Without any government or penal system, it is hard to see how such conduct can be prevented.

A second reason why this city may not be just concerns the motivational psychology of its inhabitants. As Annas argues,[14] it is significant that on Socrates' account, the primitive city's members are motivated to come together out of concern for their individual self-interests. They cannot fulfil their egoistic needs as efficiently by themselves as they can by forming alliances and making contracts with others. Hence, although the 'city of pigs' is characterized by human interdependence, there is no sense of anyone being concerned to promote any collective good over and above the satisfaction of their own individual desires. Such concern, as we shall see, is essential to Socrates' conception of political justice. Moreover, besides being purely self-interested, the inhabitants of the primitive city have a very limited conception of what their self-interest *is*. Like pigs, they seek the satisfaction of basic desires and appetites, for sufficient food and drink, shelter, physical relaxation, sex and child-rearing. There is seemingly no place for intellectual interests and no desire to possess knowledge or wisdom for its own sake, which, by contrast, forms part of Plato's conception of the just city.

We can understand, then, why Plato does not seriously consider the 'city of pigs' a candidate for justice. But, in this case, what is the basis of his comments that this city is the 'true' and 'healthy' one? Perhaps, while the primitive society does not measure up to his ideal, he still regards it as preferable to those cities where pleasure-seeking is more sophisticated. In other words, Plato might be asserting his preference for a society where sensory and aesthetic enjoyments are kept to a basic minimum – as in the ideally just city he later outlines – rather than the luxurious decadence he associates with his native Athens.

3.3.3. The need for a military

The next stage of Socrates' argument (372e–376c) enlarges the city to include the 'service' industries. These bring with them the requirement for more doctors, presumably because of the health problems caused by overindulgence, and also the need for an army, for both offensive and defensive reasons (373d). The luxurious city's land is likely to be inadequate to cater for all its population's desires, so it becomes necessary to seize neighbouring territories to secure sufficient pasture and ploughland. Moreover, other cities may wish to plunder the city's luxury goods; hence the need for military defences.

Warfare, as much as any profession, requires specialists who devote their time to it exclusively (374c–d). Those selected for this most important of roles need certain physical attributes – keen senses, speed and strength (375a), and they must also be courageous and spirited (375b). Moreover, while the ideal soldier is fierce towards the city's enemies, he will be friendly to his fellow citizens (375e). The next move is curious. From the premise that the military must distinguish between friends and enemies and treat each accordingly, Socrates derives the conclusion that its members must have a 'philosophical' nature. His argument for this is at (376b): a good guard dog, like a good soldier, decides whether someone is a friend or enemy based on whether it knows him. Those whom it knows, it regards as friends; those it does not know it treats as enemies. Hence, Socrates claims, such a being is a lover of knowledge, and thus has a philosophical (literally, knowledge-loving) bent.

This last argument cannot be taken literally. There is clearly a big difference between loving what one knows and loving knowledge *per se*; soldiers must arguably do the former but it does not follow that they must do the latter. We might, perhaps, treat Socrates' reference to a 'philosophical nature' as primarily a trailer for the thesis he will defend at length, and much more plausibly, later on: namely, that those who hold power in the city should be trained philosophers. Socrates has, anyway, established the importance of a competent military sufficiently to justify his next topic of enquiry, which concerns how those who guard the city should be educated.

Discussion questions:
(a) Socrates outlines a system where different workers specialize exclusively in certain tasks. What advantages and disadvantages might result from this practice?
(b) On what grounds do various groups in contemporary society argue for the return to a simpler and less luxurious lifestyle?

3.4. THE GUARDIANS' EDUCATION (376c–412b)

The discussion of the ideal education for the city's professional military spans the end of Book II and the first half of Book III. It focuses on two main didactic areas; first, the kinds of poetry and music it is appropriate for young 'guardians' to listen to (376c–403c), and secondly the provisions which will be made for their physical education and health (403c–412). Of these sections, the former, in particular the discussion of poetry, is the more radical and interesting, and is thus the focus of the following commentary. This passage is significant within the context of the whole of the *Republic*, moreover, as it constitutes the first of two diatribes against the literature that was popular and admired in contemporary Athens. (The second, philosophically more complex assault, is in Book X.) It is important, however, to remember that what Socrates says about poetry in Books II and III is in the specific context of outlining how guardians should be educated during their formative years. He does not, at least in these passages, make any broader claims about the censorship of art within society.

Poetry was by far the most popular kind of literature in ancient Greece, so in deciding the poems to which young guardians should be exposed, Socrates is effectively determining their literary education. The treatment of this art form in Books II and III divides into two sections. The first, (376e–392c), deals with the *content* of poetic writings; in other words, what subjects the poems studied by guardian youths should and should not concern. The second, (392c–398), is about poetic *form*; the style in which poems should and should not be composed or presented with such an audience in mind.

3.4.1. Content: propagation of falsehoods

The comments on poems' content consist largely of a string of examples from existing poetic works, primarily those of Homer, but also excerpts from Hesiod and Aeschylus. In most cases, Socrates condemns these texts as instances of a literature that is unsuitable for guardians of the just city. His criticisms are interspersed, however, with some recommendations on what the content of poems *should* be; exemplified by the odd Homeric passage of which he does approve. Running throughout this section are two concerns underlying Socrates' worries about the content of much existing poetry. The first is that he believes poetry tends to mislead its audience about matters of fact; so that, unless it is carefully censored, it is likely to imbue people with false beliefs and opinions. The second is that poetry with the 'wrong' subject matter often has a damaging effect on the characters of its students. This particularly applies to the young, where poetry forms a large part of their moral education.

It is clear, however, that Socrates sees important connections between these two lines of criticism. In his view, it is *because* much existing poetry has factually misleading content that it corrupts the souls of its students. Many of his examples bear out this point, but I shall mention just two of them here. Early in Book III, Socrates addresses Homer's descriptions of the fearful nature of the afterlife; after an individual dies, the poet suggests, his soul travels to Hades, 'lamenting its fate, leaving manhood and youth behind', where it dwells as 'a mere phantasm, with its wits completely gone'(*Iliad* 23, quoted at 386d). Now, such claims, in Socrates' words, are 'neither true nor beneficial to future warriors' (386b–c). In other words, Homer's vision of the afterlife is not only, as Socrates believes, factually incorrect, but it is also likely to invoke an excessive fear of death, making its subjects unwilling to sacrifice their lives in a noble cause, for instance on the battlefield. Hence, not only is such poetry liable to be the cause of a false belief, but this belief is itself likely to cause a defect of character, namely cowardice. And it is clearly undesirable that potential soldiers should have such a defect ingrained during their childhoods.

Another aspect of Homer which Socrates strongly condemns is his portrayal of the gods, again on the twofold grounds that it is both false and likely to encourage its audience in wrongful behaviour. One image Socrates mentions is that of Zeus, the leader of the gods, being so overcome by sexual desire for Hera that he abandons his plans and 'wants to possess [i.e. have sex with] her there on the ground' (390c–d). In Socrates' view, it is nonsense to think that a god would be subject to sexual desire; and, moreover, by propagating the untruth that the chief deity is libidinous, Homer has an adverse influence on the morals of his audience, who are likely to treat deities as role models. Someone hearing such a story will be ready to 'excuse himself' (391e) when *he* acts immoderately, on grounds that even Zeus sometimes gives way to lustful urges. Thus, again, the twin indictments of falsity and moral corruption levelled at contemporary poetry are interlinked.

On the other hand, these criticisms can be conceived of independently, and there is textual evidence that Socrates sometimes treats them as such. For example, he criticizes passages in Hesiod's *Theogony* where the gods are depicted performing cruel and immoral acts of revenge and malice (377e–388a).[15] The initial complaint about this is that such claims are instances of 'the greatest falsehood about the most important things' (377e). Socrates thinks it intrinsic to the idea of a god that he or she would not cause any evil act (379b–c); hence, part of the reason why Hesiod is deemed unsuitable is that he propagates false beliefs about the divine. But, Socrates adds, even *if* the stories about the gods' sadistic crimes were true, they should not be told to young people, because they will have a bad effect on their characters (378a–b). In particular, he argues, like many a modern censor, that exposure to such material might result in a young person being desensitized to its wickedness, regarding it as 'nothing out of the ordinary' (378b).

It is significant here that despite his general concern for promoting truth, Socrates is also willing to prohibit certain truths from being taught through poetry if they are likely to corrupt the morality of the young. Moreover, in addition to censoring true claims, Socrates seems to countenance telling untruths in order to bring about moral improvement. He says explicitly, for instance, that falsehoods expressed in literature can occasionally be useful in preventing people from committing bad acts (382c–d). We shall later examine a case where he specifically proposes propagating an untrue myth for the greater good of society.[16] Hence, promoting morality seems to supersede the concern for truth, for he is willing both to censor certain true claims, and promote false ones, because of their moral impact.

Socrates concludes his discussion of poetic content (392b) by saying that just as there are certain subject-matters which should be prohibited from didactic use, there are also some kinds of story that poets should positively be ordered to narrate. He offers few specifics, but extrapolating from what went before they will probably be tales which promote true beliefs and, most importantly, imbue virtue in those who hear them. Socrates offers the odd example of passages from existing poetry which he thinks might achieve the latter: for instance, Homer's eulogies to the Achaean warriors' courage and obedience (*Iliad* 4.443, quoted at 389e). Since, however, the majority of what Homer and other contemporary poets say is, in Socrates' eyes, damaging, we can take it that ideally he wants these authors replaced by others whose works are more likely to inspire goodness.

3.4.2. Form: the dangers of imitation

Turning from the content of poems to Socrates' discussion of their form (beginning 392c), it is important to remember that Greek poetry was predominantly written to be performed aloud at public gatherings, often to a musical accompaniment. Very rarely would poetic works be read silently in private, as is the case today. Hence, we can assume that, from Plato's perspective, the study of poetry would not have been limited to the scholarly analysis of texts, and would have involved much of what we now associate with the performing arts; learning to recite or even sing poems proficiently before an audience. The poetry of Plato's era was also invariably narrative. Socrates distinguishes (392d) between poems which narrate from a third-personal perspective outside the story itself, and those which involve explicit imitation (*mimēsis*), in which the poem's words are those of a particular character within the tale, such that whoever recites the poem speaks through the mouth of this character. In performing the latter type of poem, one is effectively 'playing a part' as in modern theatre. It is the latter, imitative brand of poetry which bears the brunt of Socrates' criticism. At (394d), he announces his intent to enquire whether any training in imitation or role-play is a suitable component of the young guardians' education, and proceeds to offer reasons why much imitative poetry should be removed from their syllabus. The first and most straightforward reason is that such training is a waste of their time and effort, and a distraction from their learning more important skills, such as defending the city (395e). This point is admissible as far as it goes, but does appear rather weak as an argument for outlawing imitative poetry in particular, since whilst the ability to recite such poetry is of limited vocational use to a soldier, the same is surely true of reciting narrative poetry written in the third-person.

A more subtle point about imitation appears at (395c–d): it is imperative, for Socrates, that guardians should not be trained to imitate base or inferior types of people (or, indeed, subhuman beings), for it is likely that 'from enjoying the imitation, they come to enjoy the reality'; '. . . imitations practised from youth', he continues, 'become part of nature and settle into habits of gesture, voice and thought' (395d). In other words, those who learn to play certain characters through reciting imitative poetry run the risk of becoming like these characters in their real-life dispositions of thought and action. This leads to Socrates placing strict limits on the types of characters who may be dramatically portrayed. Those who are 'courageous, self-controlled, pious and free' (395c) are acceptable, but those who are vicious, insane or subhuman are not (395d–396b), lest the youngsters taught to portray such parts come to acquire similar characteristics in real life.

Taken at face value, the claim that those who practise imitating certain characters will become like them seems somewhat far fetched; many an actor has played Macbeth without turning into a power-crazed murderer. The inability, on a performer's part, to separate theatrical representation from real-life conduct is surely limited to the mentally feeble, or perhaps some lunatics who mistake fantasy for reality. Annas,[17] however, offers a subtler interpretation of Socrates' point which makes it more plausible. The danger with imitating a fictional character is that the practice encourages one to identify with one's subject: to suppose oneself in his position, and imagine having his character, viewpoint, and mental states. This seems particularly the case with the techniques associated with so-called 'method' acting, where the actor seeks to conjure in himself the mindset of the character depicted. A problem therefore with playing a vicious part, from Plato's perspective, is that it involves empathizing with a value-set, actions, or a lifestyle which one should rightly find abhorrent. As empathy leads to understanding, so perhaps understanding ushers in tolerance or even sympathy. The method-actor playing a villain works out his character's reasons for thinking and acting as he does, his drives and motives, perhaps even the arguments he would use in his own defence. Once he does this, though, he effectively treats villainy as a viable, comprehensible, or even defensible way of life. And it is counterproductive, Plato might believe, for young soldiers to be trained to view vice in this way; rather, they should meet it with condemnation and anger.

Socrates' prohibitions on imitation are not limited to the portrayal of villains, but encompass also women, slaves, working-class men, animals and inanimate objects. Trainee guardians should never imitate 'neighing horses, bellowing bulls, roaring rivers, the crashing sea, (or) thunder', on grounds that 'they are forbidden to be mad or imitate mad people' (396b). Here, the problem seems less one of empathizing with an *ethically* corrupt viewpoint, than of giving vent to one's passions by imitating non-rational things, invoking elemental drives and expressing them in sound or movement. As we shall see later, it is vitally important to Socrates' just city that those who occupy its senior posts think and act in accordance with reason, and that their passionate and primeval attributes are kept firmly in check. Pretending to be an animal, or a storm at sea, involves giving free rein to the lower, non-rational elements of one's soul – indeed it is akin to behaving insanely – and it is thus quite the wrong type of formative experience for a future civic leader, in whom wisdom and intellectual qualities should be foremost. In a similar way, the imitation of humans who are deemed less than fully rational – women, slaves, and so on – is considered unconducive to reason's development.

Socrates concludes (396c–e) that imitation in poetry must be kept to a minimum, and the characters imitated should predominantly be virtuous and rational. This, he believes, will best contribute to the guardians' training as soldiers and as potential leaders of the city. Of course, there are various grounds on which one might disagree with either Socrates' ends or his means. First, one might dispute his conception of the ideal political leader as a rational individual who abnegates passion and instinct. Secondly, one could deny that training in role-play has the corrupting tendencies he suggests, pointing instead to its potential merits, perhaps in promoting understanding of a wide range of human psychologies, and indeed coming to terms with the more primal elements within oneself. But even if we grant Socrates' ultimate aims and his views about the psychological impacts of poetry, his specific prescriptions are open to debate. For example, if the problem with imitation is that it encourages empathy with the wrong types of character (following Annas' reading), then might not such empathy also be induced by the non-imitative, third-personal type of poetry? Equally, we might wonder why Socrates' focus is solely on the effects of poetry on those who *recite* it, and not on members of its audience, who could surely also be seduced into identifying with inappropriate character-types.[18]

It is questionable, then, whether Socrates succeeds in justifying his invective against imitative poetry and its impact upon its performers. In essence, however, his underlying point about the guardians' poetic education is a plausible one, with which almost all would agree; namely that the texts to which people are exposed as youngsters have significant impacts not only on their beliefs, but on the general formation of their characters. The notion that some censorship should therefore be applied to the young is, likewise, relatively commonplace. How many, even within modern-day society, would oppose limitations on the films children can attend or the books they read? As will become clear, moreover, Socrates' specific emphasis on moulding the characters of the guardians, as opposed to citizens in general, will be justified by the immensely responsible roles he expects them to fulfil within the ideal city.

I shall pass over Socrates' remarks on the guardians' schooling in music (398c–403c) and their physical education and diet (beginning 403c), and move on to consider how he makes use of this carefully trained group within the organization of the just state.

Discussion questions:

(a) Do certain kinds of literature implant false beliefs? Is this an important concern as regards the literary education of children?

(b) Is the danger of people empathizing with fictional characters, or treating them as role models, a good reason for censoring certain works?

3.5. THE IDEAL STATE (412b–434c)

3.5.1. Lifestyle and powers of rulers

At (412b), Socrates returns to the question of how the just city should be structured. Its educated elite, he says, should be subdivided into two classes. The superior class comprises those who, having attained sufficient years, are entrusted with the overall government of the city. Those in the lesser group function as auxiliaries; their main role is military combat, under the orders of the first, who are subsequently referred to as 'complete guardians' (414b). The selection of the ruling class will be determined by a test of knowledge and abilities (412c) as well as commitment to promoting the city's interests, which ideally a guardian should identify with his or her own (412d). Once in place, moreover, the rulers' lifestyles will be strictly regulated. They will not be permitted any significant private income or wealth, but will live in public accommodation and attend common meals (416d–e). Later, in Book V, it emerges that they may neither marry nor have families.

The main justification for denying the guardians private financial interests is to lessen the likelihood of their abusing power to further their finances. A ruler who is allowed wealth acquisition might swiftly become a 'household manager' (417a), more concerned with his own affluence than the well-being of the state. Equally, wealthy rulers could invoke envy among the masses and be subject to plots and rebellions. A further reason for denying luxury to government officials is offered later in Book IV (421e); such pleasures, it is claimed, are addictive, and will distract the guardians, as they would any worker, from the tasks they are bound to carry out. Obviously, if a *ruler* is thus distracted, the consequences for the whole city will be particularly catastrophic.

Socrates' guidelines for the treatment of political leaders are radical by most standards, and are open to the following powerful objection: if the leaders of society are forced to live frugally and denied a private life, what exactly motivates them to govern efficiently? Will they not rather be demoralized and made resentful by their relative poverty? This may well be the point of the question Adeimantus poses at the start of Book IV (419), where he asks how Socrates would respond to the complaint that his system fails to ensure the happiness of the city's ruling class. Socrates' response, however, is twofold. First, he comments (420b) that it is not clear that guardians living under such communistic conditions *are* unhappy, the implication being that this depends on one's account of happiness (a topic he will address later). Secondly, the aim in constructing a just city should not be 'to make any one group outstandingly happy but to make the whole city so' (420b). Using an attractive metaphor, Socrates argues that just as a sculptor, in making a statue, does not focus solely on the beauty of its most attractive part (say, its eyes) but rather utilizes this part to promote the beauty of the whole, so the ideal city should be arranged not merely to render its leading citizens happy, but to bring about the happiness of the entire civic body: 'the city as a whole' (421b).

The meaning of Socrates' talk of a city, as opposed to the individuals within it, being happy, has led to significant criticisms of his political thought, which will be addressed in section 3.5.3. Before this, I shall take stock of the civic constitution Plato proposes, and the virtues he believes it will enshrine.

3.5.2. The city and its virtues

The city is to be pyramidically structured with three classes of citizens: the guardians, who rule; the auxiliaries, who engage in warfare; and the remainder, a 'productive' class of craftsmen, farmers and other workers. Membership of the two higher classes is, we may assume, determined by the rigorous testing procedure outlined at (414d–414a). There is a clear indication (415a–b), however, that in Socrates' view the children of guardian parents are most likely to qualify for a similar status, and likewise with the other social groups. And indeed, in Book V, he spells out a eugenic programme designed to breed the best possible guardians by bringing together illustrious parents, thus confirming a belief in the largely hereditary nature of intellectual and other human abilities. He does also admit that in some circumstances young people may show merit significantly above or below what one might expect given their birth, and that in these cases they should be placed in the class appropriate to their talents. Hence, while there appears little or no social mobility for citizens of

Socrates' state once they are assigned to a class, his system does at least seek to select on the basis of merit rather than birth alone.

To help ensure universal acceptance of this stratified arrangement, Socrates suggests a myth should be propagated to the effect that membership of the three classes was divinely preordained. Each citizen, according to this legend, was mixed, before his or her birth, with a different metal: gold in the case of the guardian rulers, silver for the auxiliaries, and iron and bronze for the working class (415a). The propagation of this story constitutes, in Socrates' words, a 'noble falsehood' (414b), and here we witness his concern for truth (as discussed in section 3.4.1) being overridden by his commitment to social stability. The 'myth of the metals' should, if universally believed, encourage every citizen to accept their station in society as determined by their essential nature. The working class will submit to be ruled by others, while the guardians and auxiliaries will tolerate their frugal living conditions on the assurance that 'they always have gold and silver of a divine sort in their souls' (416e). As an aside, it does seem odd that even the highly educated ruling class is, on Socrates' recommendation, to be fed untrue propaganda to ensure their compliance. After all, one might expect that given their supposed wisdom, they would be capable of seeing for themselves that it best befits society for them to govern and live as this system dictates.

It is argued that there should be no legislation built into the city's constitution over such matters as contracts, employment, lawsuits, establishment of juries, taxation, or the regulation of civic institutions (425c–d). Such constraints would unduly tie the hands of the guardians, who, in Socrates' view, should be given absolute freedom to determine policy and amend rules as they see fit. As Socrates states (427a), detailed constitutional constraints are unnecessary given a competent and properly trained set of leaders, and pointless if the city is poorly governed, as they will not adequately compensate for the rulers' failings. His proposal for the ideal city, then, is for absolute political power in the hands of a trained ruling class, the only exception being over questions of revealed religious law (427b).

Having laid out the structure of his state, Socrates proceeds to identify and characterize its virtues. At (427e) he enumerates four: wisdom, courage, moderation and, most important, justice. He then details each virtue in turn. Wisdom, when ascribed to a political community, refers to the knowledge possessed by its ruling class (428b–429a). The wise city is one where those who take major decisions of state are themselves wise and knowledgeable. The knowledge that soldiers and craftsmen have in their fields of endeavour, while no doubt beneficial to the city, does not determine whether *it*, as a whole, is deemed wise. The city's courage, by contrast, consists in the bravery possessed by its warrior class (429b–430c). A city is courageous if its soldiers display appropriate steadfastness; again, whether or not other members of the state are also resilient is irrelevant to assessing the *city*'s courage.

The first two virtues of the state, then, involve qualities of particular classes of citizens – rulers and soldiers respectively – and Socrates' educational system is meant to ensure that these qualities are strong. The third virtue, moderation, is different insofar as it is said to involve 'consonance and harmony' (430e) *between* different social classes. It is defined in terms of the ruling class controlling the behaviour of the 'inferior majority' (431c), and the majority acquiescing to such rule; 'sharing the same belief' that their lives should be governed by those trained to promote the city's interests (431d–e). We have here one of the first expositions of a common theme of the political sections of the *Republic*, namely that the city's productive workers are unfit to exercise any power within the state and should submit completely to the guardians' authority. In the so-called moderate city, the lower class fully consents to this subordinate position.

Socrates' next project, having defined three virtues, is to analyse justice in the political context. Looking back to (427e–428a), we see that his method of doing so is first to analyse all the other named virtues of the ideal state, and then to consider which of its acknowledged qualities has not yet been included. These other virtues, it transpires, are the three already outlined – wisdom, courage and moderation. This argumentative method appears somewhat suspect, since there is no *a priori* reason to think that the state's virtues should be limited to four, or that the qualities delineated under the terms 'wisdom', 'courage' and 'moderation' necessarily encompass all but one virtuous aspect of the ideal city.[19]

In Socrates' view, however, there is just one further virtue worthy of a label, which he says has been 'at our feet from the very beginning' (432d). This – the essence of justice – is the system whereby each member of the ideal state 'does their own' (433b); that is, carries out the task which their station in society defines for them. In particular, it is vital for justice that no one attempts the work of members of a class other than his own, especially a class above it. No craftsman, then, should practise soldiering, and no soldier should take on a ruler's position; if there is 'meddling and exchange' between the three classes, this causes 'the greatest harm that can happen to a city', and amounts, on Socrates' conception, to injustice (434b). The possibility of different members of the productive class doing each others' designated jobs is also mentioned (434a), with cases of a carpenter doing the work of a cobbler or vice versa; but, while discouraged, this is deemed to cause 'not much' harm and is not specifically regarded as unjust. Instances of members of a higher class doing the work of a lower one are not considered at all. However, the final definition of justice in the city (434c), which involves 'the money-making, auxiliary, and guardian classes each to do its own work', suggests that such practices would undermine the virtue.

It is questionable to what extent Plato's account of political justice is clearly distinguished from what he calls moderation. There appears, at least, to be an overlap between the concepts: moderation involves the rulers ruling over their inferiors, and justice encompasses the guardian class carrying out its allotted task, namely to govern. Both virtues, however, have certain nuances which are absent from the other. Moderation is partly characterized by the *willing* submission of the productive class, which is not mentioned when justice is discussed, whereas justice defines positive functions in society for both auxiliaries and producers, which are not relevant to moderation. The virtues are, then, appreciably distinct, although both incorporate the notion of the educated guardians being solely responsible for government.

3.5.3. Objections to Plato's system

I shall now consider two very different types of objection that might be levelled at Plato's account of the ideal state. The first specifically concerns the account of political justice Socrates proposes, whilst the second challenges his entire conception of the virtuous city.

A definition of political justice as expressed in each citizen fulfilling his or her designated role can be questioned on grounds that this account seems far removed from what 'justice' is ordinarily taken to mean. When most of us speak of justice in the context of a state, the quality we have in mind is considerably different from the one Socrates identifies. It might, then, be argued that whether or not Socrates is right to think that each citizen 'doing his own work' is a civic virtue, this is a different phenomenon from the virtue of justice.

In particular, there are certain widely recognized features of justice which Socrates' definition omits. These include, for example, its distributive aspect. Intuitively, the question of whether a city's goods and resources are distributed among its citizens fairly or according to desert is relevant to whether or not the city is just. Also, it is commonly thought that one element of a state's justice concerns its behaviour towards other states. A city whose external policy is to despoil and pillage its neighbours, for example, could be called unjust, regardless of whether its citizens do the jobs allocated to them. Socrates' account seems to ignore this point.

There is no direct indication of how Plato might have responded to these arguments, so we need to extrapolate an answer from his stated views. One possible way to reconcile Socrates' account of justice with more common conceptions of the notion, suggested by Annas,[20] is to see the practice of each citizen performing his allocated task as *leading to* a state that is just in more conventional ways; including, perhaps, those of organizing a fair internal distribution of resources and following a scrupulous foreign policy. The means by which this might occur is via the guardian class ensuring that the policies they enact are just in the conventional sense. Hence, a state which is just by Socrates' definition – ruled by those trained and best suited for the task – will, through its government's actions, enjoy fair allocations of goods and ethical relationships with other cities. Indeed, Plato could go further and claim that *only* when government is restricted to the appropriate class of citizen will conventionally just policies prevail. If the less able or less well-trained take over, unfair or rapacious policies might well ensue.

There is specific mention in the text, at (433e), of the idea that a state organized along the lines Socrates calls 'just' will lead to what is more commonly understood as a just society. Here, Socrates argues that provided the judges in the city's courts are drawn from the carefully selected and educated guardian class, then the aim of such people in delivering judgements will be 'that no citizen should have what belongs to another or be deprived of their own' (ibid.). In other words, they will follow principles of fairness with regard to property. Hence, justice in the Socratic sense of appropriate allocation of tasks *contributes* to justice in a more familiar sense, namely respect for property in legal verdicts.

If Socratic justice provides the conditions for conventional justice to prosper, it is also possible to impute a relationship in the other direction, whereby certain aspects of conventional justice are necessary as a backdrop for justice in the Socratic sense. In particular, consider Socrates' words at (423e): he claims that if a city is too unequal in the distribution of wealth among its citizens, it will suffer internal division, becoming effectively 'two cities at war with one another, that of the poor and that of the rich'. When a state is divided in this way, moreover, it can be more easily attacked from outside, since the enemy can ally itself with one of the factions – most likely the poor – in order to overthrow the other. These arguments suggest that a relatively equal distribution of resources, often regarded as a central feature of political justice, is valued by Socrates as a means to sustaining his ideal society. In particular, it seems highly unlikely that justice in Socrates' sense – each citizen working at their allotted task – will be achievable without a certain measure of economic equality among the citizens. If such equality is absent, then the citizens will focus not on their assigned roles, but on furthering their sectional interests as members of a 'rich' or 'poor' class, or, in extreme cases, seeking to uproot the entire social structure through alliances with outsiders. Thus again, while Socrates' account of justice differs from the norm, it may go hand in hand with an important element of justice as conventionally conceived – relative equality of resources – without which, Plato believes, there is little hope of individuals staying loyal to their prescribed vocations.

In addition to questions about Plato's specific account of political justice, he has frequently been subjected to a more general criticism, usually from a liberal democratic standpoint, that he advocates an effectively totalitarian system of government. In his ideal political regime, it is argued, individuals' lives are subject to an unpalatable degree of state control, and, on some interpretations, their welfare is sacrificed for the greater good of the city.

It is important to separate different strands in the possible liberal objections to Plato's political arrangements. C. C. W. Taylor (1999) distinguishes three different charges. The first, over which there can be little doubt, is that Plato is a *paternalist*, who believes the state is justified in making decisions on behalf of its ordinary citizens, many of whom he considers incapable of deciding what is best for themselves.[21] This is strongly implied, for example, in the account of moderation, in which 'the desires of the inferior many are controlled by the wisdom and desires of the superior few' (431c–d). Support for paternalism need not, however, imply that the state is unconcerned for the happiness of its citizens. One might, after all, see the guardians' control of the productive class as promoting the latter's own interests. If the producers are so unruly and uneducable that they cannot identify what is good for them, and the guardians know this better, then allowing the guardians to determine the producers' behaviour will actually increase the producers' well-being. Hence, while the idea of denying human beings freedom to determine their own actions and plans of life, on grounds that they cannot choose wisely for themselves, may be opposed in many liberal quarters,[22] it is not the same thing as sacrificing individual interests altogether.

A second 'illiberal' view, which Plato could be taken to hold, is that individual citizens' welfare is best promoted by devoting themselves entirely to working for the good of the city. According to such a view, the best and happiest condition for an individual is to contribute to the collective good of his state, rather than seeking to further his private well-being or those of his family or friends. Such a position has echoes in the political thought of Jean-Jacques Rousseau, who argues that it is only when a citizen subjugates his 'private will' to the 'general will' to promote the common good that he becomes truly free.[23] Taylor, however, argues that there is limited evidence on which to ascribe this position to Plato.[24] Admittedly, there is one passage (420b) where Socrates says that it would 'not be surprising' if the guardians were happiest renouncing private wealth and families to devote themselves to furthering the city's interests. But when he later proposes that political justice involves each citizen 'doing his own' allotted task for the collective good, he never suggests that such a course makes them individually happy. Hence, if Plato strongly believed that the greatest happiness for an individual involved performing public works, we might expect him to advertise this point more.

The third and most serious charge of totalitarianism levelled at Plato is that he values the interests of the state as an entity over and above the welfare of individuals, and that consequently he is willing to overlook individual interests in pursuit of the wider goals attributed to the city *per se*. According to Karl Popper,[25] Plato subscribes to a 'general principle of collectivism' under which the individual is made to 'subserve the interests of the state as a whole'. Passages which might imply this include Socrates' response to Adeimantus' objection that the guardians' communistic living conditions will not make them happy. Socrates replies that the ultimate aim of his system is not to further the happiness of individual groups of citizens, but rather that of the whole state (420b). Later, moreover, he states that his purpose, in constructing a constitution for the ideal state, is 'to see that the city *as a whole* has the greatest happiness' (421b).

These passages raise the question of what exactly Plato means when he speaks of a city, as opposed to individual people, being (or failing to be) happy.[26] He is sometimes accused of seeing the state as like a living organism, with its citizens comprising the organs of its body.[27] The danger with such a view, from a liberal perspective, is that the organic state might have interests of its own which potentially conflict with those of the individual people within it, and which may indeed be given priority over these individuals' welfare. There is, however, a possible move which avoids this implication and coheres instead with the utilitarian principles of philosophers such as Jeremy Bentham and John Stuart Mill. This is to regard the city's happiness as the aggregate sum of the happiness of each individual citizen. On such an account, the point of, say, compelling the guardians to live communally would be to ensure the maximum amount of individual happiness throughout the state. Whilst the guardians themselves may suffer from their living conditions, this unhappiness is more than counterbalanced, in the overall calculus, by the happiness which these conditions afford others – perhaps because the rulers govern more efficiently as a result of being thus accommodated.

This account of the city's happiness is unlikely to silence Plato's liberal critics, who may object to the idea of it being legitimate, in pursuit of maximum aggregate utility, to trade off the happiness of some individuals for the greater happiness of others. This, they might claim, involves exploiting the former group, using them as a means to promote others' interests and denying them appropriate consideration as individuals in their own right; indeed, many philosophers object to utilitarianism along precisely these lines.[28] Despite this, however, the proposed account at least makes the city's welfare dependent on the individual human welfare within its borders, thereby avoiding any more elaborate notion of the city as a super-person with independent interests of its own.

Discussion questions:

(a) In Plato's moderate city, ordinary citizens unquestioningly accept their leaders' decisions and orders. What are the dangers of such acquiescence, and in what circumstances is it permissible or even obligatory to disobey one's rulers?

(b) Evaluate the idea that the state should compel its citizens to do what is in their own best interest.

3.6. THE SOUL AND ITS VIRTUES (434d–445e)

The second half of Book IV modulates from the political to the personal sphere, as Socrates develops accounts of the parts of the individual soul and its virtues, analogous to his treatment of the state. The Greek term usually translated as soul is *psuchē*. This word has none of the religious or spiritual connotations we often associate with a soul, and neither does it necessarily suggest an immaterial substance distinct from the body, as famously postulated by Descartes. A *psuchē* is essentially a feature of a living thing – the Greeks commonly believed that every animal possesses one, as indeed, in Aristotle's view, do all plants. Plato's discussion in the *Republic*, however, is exclusively concerned with the *human* soul, a phenomenon broadly equivalent to what we might term the mind or mentality. Human souls, according to Plato, consist of three parts: the rational (*logistikon*), the spirited (*thumoeidēs*) and the appetitive (*epithumētikon*). The nature and individuation of these parts is explored in the section of *Republic* IV spanning (435) to (441).

3.6.1. The soul's division

Socrates offers three lines of argument to suggest that a human soul is divided into three. The first (435a–c) involves a simple analogy between political and individual virtue. The four virtues identified earlier in Book IV – justice, wisdom, courage and moderation – are properties which both cities and individual souls can possess. According to Socrates, the political manifestations of these virtues presuppose the city's division into three parts – rulers, soldiers and productive workers. The virtues themselves involve either the successful operation of one or more of these parts, or, in the case of moderation, a certain relationship between them. Now, if the synonymous virtues in the soul are analogous to those of the state, they presumably must involve similar operations of, and relations between, different parts of the soul; and for the analogy to hold fully there must be three such parts. This said, Socrates acknowledges that we must not assume the soul is divided along similar lines to the state simply because their virtues have similar names; on the contrary '. . . if something different is found in the individual, then we must go back and test that on the city' (434e). He is committed, then, to seeking evidence, independent of the state-soul analogy, for the soul's tripartite division.

The second argument for the three-part soul (435e) begins to assemble such evidence. The different characteristics that cities can have, Socrates argues, issue from the different psychological attributes of the individuals living there. For instance, the warlike nature of certain cities results from the spiritedness or aggression of people within them, and the love of learning typical of Athens stems from the intellectual interests of (some) Athenian citizens.

This argument is followed swiftly by another, more detailed (436b–439e), which is based on what Cross and Woozley[29] term the 'principle of conflict'. This principle, as stated at (436b), says that 'the same thing will not be willing to do or undergo opposites in the same part of itself in relation to the same thing, at the same time'. An example follows: if a man stands on a spot but is moving his hands and head, we should not say that he, as a whole, is both moving and stationary, since these properties are opposite, and therefore incompatible when ascribed to the same thing. Instead, we should say that some parts of the man (legs and torso) are stationary, while others (arms and head) are moving, thereby dissolving any inconsistency. More generally, when an object appears to possess two opposing properties at once, possible contradictions must be avoided by ascribing the properties to two different component parts. Socrates applies this principle to the soul in cases of conflict of motivation. Suppose for example that someone is thirsty, but nonetheless desists from drinking (439b–d). Applying Socrates' rule, we should not say that this person, as a whole, simultaneously wants to drink and wants not to drink. Rather, we should say that some part of him, namely his thirst, desires drink, and that another part, one involving 'rational calculation' (439c), desires the contrary. The fact that these motives are in conflict establishes, Socrates believes, their existence in different parts of the human soul (439d); in this case, an *appetitive* part and a *rational* one respectively.

This distinction between reason (*logos*) and appetite (*epithumia*) raises several interesting points. First, it is significant that Plato assigns reason the capacity to motivate certain courses of action on its own. This implies that Platonic reason contains what we might, in a broad sense, term *desire* – that is, the motivational drive to pursue or avoid certain ends or actions. This account of reason stands in sharp contrast with a renowned alternative view, associated with the philosopher David Hume, which holds that reason is motivationally inert. On Hume's account, reason does not itself give rise to any desires, but merely provides information about the best means to fulfilling them. Hence, on a Humean view, it is impossible for reason itself to oppose the impulse given by a passion or appetite[30] in the way Socrates describes reason opposing thirst with a rationally grounded desire to eschew drinking.

For Plato, then, reason does more than merely judge and calculate; it also supplies the motivational force underlying certain acts. This raises the question of what kind of motivations fall under reason's auspices. The text of Book IV is not altogether clear on this point, though it seems that the person who desists from drinking with a 'rational' motive might be conceived as acting prudentially, perhaps because he suspects that the particular liquid before him is unhealthy, or because he has short supplies of drink and wishes to preserve them. In this case, reason's motive is to do what is considered best once having taken all factors, including future events, into consideration.[31] There are other passages, however, where the goals whose pursuit reason is said to motivate are more specifically associated with *intellectual* activity; ends such as knowledge and learning (see Book IX, 581b). It seems, then, that Platonic reason incorporates a range of motives, some of which involve practical calculations of what is best, as in the drink example, while others enshrine an affinity with intellectual or academic pursuits.[32]

We might seek further to clarify the nature of rational motives by contrast with appetitive ones. Appetite, in Socrates' words, is the part of a human being which 'lusts, hungers, thirsts and gets excited', and is 'a companion of certain indulgences and pleasures' (439d). It can thus safely be said to include bodily desires for such ends as food, drink and sex, together with tastes for more sophisticated forms of sensory gratification, like those derived from perfumes or massages. The category of appetite also seems, however, to contain some less physically-oriented motives; for instance the desire for money (see 580d–581a). Another significant point about appetite is made at (438a): appetites such as hunger and thirst do not necessitate conceiving of their objects as 'good'. A thirsty person, for instance, may desire a drink, and have no thoughts concerning whether the drink in question is a good one (to coin an example, someone in the grip of thirst might swallow dirty water – or worse – in order to satisfy his appetite). This suggests another possible distinction between rational and appetitive motives: the former, or at least many of them, involve thoughts about the goodness of objects, actions, events or situations, whereas the latter involve no such conceptualization.

The notion that appetite involves desiring an object without conceiving it as good is also significant within the context of Plato's wider philosophy, as it apparently conflicts with the position he sets out in a passage of his earlier dialogue, the *Meno*. There (77b–78b), Socrates argues to the effect that everything an individual desires, he must believe to be good – a claim which appears to have been dropped by the time of the *Republic*. The revision of this view furnishes Plato with an altogether more plausible account of wrongful action; for if, as the *Meno* argument implied, everything we desire we regard as somehow good, the only sense one might make of someone voluntarily pursuing a bad end, such as murder or adultery, is that he mistakenly regards it as a good one. Once we acknowledge that one can be motivated by appetite to pursue something one does *not* believe good, we can explain some such actions as being performed with the agent's full knowledge that the desired objective is bad. This phenomenon of *akrasia*, of doing something one knows, rationally, to be wrong or inadvisable, is discussed at some length by Aristotle, and has been much debated by subsequent philosophers of mind.[33] The *Republic*'s account of appetite is a first step towards allowing for its existence.

Having distinguished reason from appetite using the principle of conflict, Plato employs the same principle (439e–441c) to demarcate a third element of the soul, one comprising spirit (*thumos*). The first example he gives is the story of Leontius, who, while walking outside the Athenian walls, comes across a pile of bodies – corpses of those recently executed. The sight produces in him a conflict of desires. On the one hand, an unnamed appetite, possibly a morbid fascination with decay, or perhaps even necrophilia, tempts him to take a closer look. But on the other hand, he feels disgusted and angry at himself for having such appetites, and these passions urge him to avert his eyes. The latter motive, which conflicts with his appetite, is characterized by Socrates as a species of spirit. It is not, Socrates claims, simply the voice of Leontius' reason, though it does ally itself with his rational faculty (440a), which also advocates retreating from the scene. In this case, then, reason and spirit are both opposed to appetite, which alone desires a closer examination of the bodies. Reason and spirit are not the same, however, because in other instances they conflict with each other, for example in the case of someone who is irrationally angry (see 441b–c). In this case, while spirit desires to take revenge against a perceived enemy, reason, taking a more prudent view, counsels calm and restraint. The fact that spirit opposes reason in certain cases is enough, according to the principle of conflict, to distinguish them as separate parts of the soul. However, Socrates also offers another argument for the distinction (440a–b), based on the fact that the souls of small children and non-human animals may contain elements of spirit, even though rationality has not yet developed in the former and is never present in the latter. Since spirit can exist in non-rational souls, Socrates claims, it must be different from reason.

We might, again, question exactly what kinds of motivation fall under spirit's auspices. Socrates' examples suggest various species of anger: from self-directed annoyance at one's own weaknesses (439e–440a); through righteous anger at perceived injustice, such as we might term indignation (440c–d); to the instinctive aggression of animals (441b). There are, moreover, some instances of spirit which do not seem to involve anger at all. In Book IX, for instance, Socrates describes the spirited part of the soul as desiring 'control, victory, and high repute' (581a–b). This suggests that pride and self-esteem, as well as anger, fall into this psychological category. Is a unified account of spirit (*thumos*) possible? It does appear that all the motives it encompasses involve some kind of emotion, though clearly not all emotions are elements of *thumos*; extreme terror, and romantic love, for example, do not fit the bill. Annas[34] suggests that the mental states grouped into this category are linked by two factors: first, concern for the self and its status, and second, an ideal, which may have either been achieved, for instance in pride; or not, as in anger and shame. While, however, this characterization covers most of the cases mentioned in the text, it seems less applicable to that of dumb animals, which are explicitly said (441b) to have spirit, but which surely both lack the self-consciousness and capacity to formulate ideals, which Annas' account deems essential.[35]

There are difficulties, then, in pinpointing exactly what constitutes spirit, as was the case with reason and to a lesser extent appetite.

There are also more general problems with Plato's attempt to divide the soul into parts. A major question concerns the principle of conflict. According to this principle, the fact that two motivations conflict is sufficient to place them in different sections of the soul. It is unclear, however, how Plato would respond to cases where people experience conflicts between motives that would most naturally be placed into the same category. Take, for example, someone who is both hungry and thirsty at once, and who is therefore torn between eating and drinking. Or take a student who enjoys both philosophy and theoretical physics, wants to attend lectures in both subjects, but is unable to because their times coincide. It would make sense to say that the former has a conflict between two appetites, for food and drink, while the latter experiences two contrary motives from within the category of reason, both involving a love of learning. But if this is so, then contrary to the principle of conflict, the opposition between two motives is not sufficient to distinguish them as belonging to different parts of the soul.[36] Plato could of course appeal to other psychological features of these motives to determine their respective categories; but if he does so, then not only does the principle of conflict seem redundant, but it becomes even more important that the criteria for mental states being appetitive, spirited, or rational are clearly defined. Plato's own accounts of them, however, are anecdotal and somewhat opaque.

Another question is whether Plato intends his three faculties of soul to incorporate *every* motive it is possible to undergo. It might be argued that some widely recognized motivational states do not obviously fall into any of the three pigeonholes. Is the fear of danger an appetite? Is pity a rational state, or a non-standard manifestation of spirit? What about an urge towards artistic creativity, or the desire for intimacy with a close friend or relative? It is difficult to see how the three categories Plato labels 'reason', 'spirit', and 'appetite' can plausibly be framed so as to exhaust the entire range of possible human motives.

Despite these criticisms, Plato's attempt to categorize parts of the soul constitutes an interesting foray into psychology, and is a platform for more detailed and involved taxonomies of virtues and emotions, such as those later attempted by Aristotle.[37] Within the *Republic*, moreover, the soul's tripartite division plays the pivotal role of establishing an analogy between the individual soul and the political state. According to this model, the soul's rational element is the psychological corollary of the guardian class in the city; the spirited part is analogous to the militaristic auxiliaries; and the diverse appetites correspond to the various productive craftsmen and traders.

3.6.2. Virtues of character

Plato's next topic (441c–444c) is to extend his analogy to outline the soul's four virtues. These are defined in terms of functionings of, or relations between, the parts of the soul, which, as we shall see, almost exactly parallel the operations of the different classes involved in the virtues of the state. This analogy works specifically as follows:

a. **Wisdom** (442c): in the soul, this involves the rational part making knowledgeable decisions about which courses of action are advantageous. (In political terms, similarly, it involved the guardians knowledgeably determining what is best for the city as a whole).

b. **Courage** (442b): in an individual, this involves spirit providing the steadfastness needed to enact the decisions reason has made, either in the face of pain or under temptation by pleasure. For example, if Leontius overcame his appetite to look at the corpses because of the urgings of his spirit, such restraint would constitute courage. The same, presumably, applies to someone whose spirit motivates him to do what he believes best in spite of danger. In the state, again correspondingly, courage consists in the resolve of the auxiliary class in executing the guardians' orders.

c. **Moderation** (442d): as an individual virtue, this consists in a 'friendly and harmonious relation' between the soul's parts, in which all of them 'believe in common that the rational part should rule and do not engage in civil war against it' (ibid.). This again parallels the earlier account of political moderation, which entailed the soldiers and producers willingly accepting rule by the guardians.

There is a problem, regarding the individual virtue of moderation, about *how* passions and appetites are able to 'accept' the rule of reason. Some appetites are nothing more than bodily urges such as hunger and thirst. To describe these drives as 'holding beliefs' that they should be under rational control seems a curious personification, which perhaps pushes the analogy with the state too far. It might be claimed, however, that this is intended merely figuratively, to refer to a harmony between reason and the other parts of the soul, in which neither appetite nor spirit offers any motivation to conflict with those of reason. So, for example, the moderate person's appetite for food will be such that he feels hunger only for what he rationally believes is good for him. Likewise, his spirit is so constituted as to feel anger only when he reasons that an aggressive course is justified, and so forth.

d. **Justice** (441e–442a): like a city, a soul is just when each of its parts 'does its own work'. Reason's task is to determine action, in the same way as the guardians direct the state's activities. Spirit is charged with being reason's 'ally' (441e), helping to execute the acts reason dictates, as soldiers do for their political masters. Examples are unfortunately lacking here, but we might perhaps imagine that when a just person has rationally decided it is best to confront an enemy, his spirit, in the form of a controlled anger at the enemy's behaviour, helps motivate him to carry out the confrontation.

The proper function of appetite (442a) is characterized in passive terms: like the productive class, it must be governed by the soul's other parts, becoming neither too strong nor too independent. Socrates does not mention any more positive role for appetite than this, though we might surmise that, just as producers provide for the material needs of the city, appetite's function is to ensure the individual's physical well-being by reminding him when his body requires nutrition or sustenance.

The end of Book IV sees the beginning of Socrates' response to the challenge he was set by Glaucon and Adeimantus, namely to show that justice is a good worth having in itself, not merely for its consequences, nor indeed for the advantages of simply appearing to be just. Now that Socrates has defined justice as a virtue of an individual soul, he believes himself in a position to answer this question. The method by which he initially does so is by introducing yet another analogy, this time between justice, as 'a kind of health, fine condition, and well-being of the soul' (444d–e), and health in a physical body. It is significant that he refers to health here, since the same property was used, back in Book II (357c), as an example of a good that is valuable both intrinsically and for its consequences – the category into which Socrates also places justice. In a physically healthy individual, it is claimed, 'the components of the body are in a natural relation of control and being controlled, one by another' (444d). In disease, by contrast, the interactions between the body's parts are unnatural. Similarly, when a soul is just, its components exhibit the natural relation of 'ruling and being ruled' (ibid.) with reason in charge of spirit and appetite; when unjust, the soul's internal power-relations are unnatural ones, with some non-rational part(s) usurping the proper function of reason.

If, as this suggests, justice is to the soul as health is to the body, it seems to follow intuitively that it is a property worth possessing from the perspective of the just agent's well-being. It would be 'ridiculous', Glaucon agrees (445a), for someone to desire an *un*natural ordering of his soul, which is 'the very thing by which he lives' (445b), even if such an ordering granted him a wealth of worldly goods. Hence someone like Gyges, who sacrifices justice in pursuit of riches and power, thereby deprives himself of something far more important, namely the internal harmony and good psychological order in which justice consists. His body may or may not fare well in the luxurious life he builds for himself. His soul, undoubtedly, is 'ruined and in turmoil' (ibid.).

3.6.3. Problems with Plato's arguments

Passages like the above have undoubted rhetorical appeal, but careful consideration might lead us to wonder whether Socrates has performed a clever sleight of hand in his effort to render justice appealing. In particular, he stands accused by critics such as David Sachs (1963), of a 'fallacy of irrelevance',[38] in which he defends justice against its would be detractors by altering the meaning of the term. It is worth examining this charge, and possible defences Plato might have against it, at some length.

In Book II, when Glaucon and Adeimantus laid out the problem faced by those defending the just life, the conception of justice underpinning their arguments appeared to be a broadly conventional one. In the Ring of Gyges story, the shepherd's unjust conduct consisted in deceit, adultery, murder, and usurpment. Correspondingly, it would seem that 'justice' was being assumed to refer to the opposites of such acts: truth telling and respect for the persons, property and relationships of others. Indeed, this much was clearly stated at (360b–c), where the just man was described as someone who refrains from such activities as exploitation and defrauding of others. This 'conventional' account of justice has two main features which distinguish it from the alternative conception outlined by Socrates. First, conventional justice concerns relations between individuals: one's treatment of others and response to their interests. Second, justice is conventionally taken to be a function of the way an individual *acts*, rather than his internal psychological states.[39] It is significant, for instance, that the description of Gyges' injustice is framed exclusively in terms of his behaviour rather than his beliefs and desires.

By defining justice as a psychological phenomenon – an ordering of elements within the soul – and arguing that such an ordering is valuable for the individual concerned, it might be claimed that Socrates fails to answer the question he was originally posed. He was asked to show why justice, in the conventional sense in which Glaucon and Adeimantus understood it, was a good worth pursuing in and of itself. He has responded, however, by showing why justice *in a quite different sense* is valuable. This, then, is the 'irrelevance' of which Sachs accuses him; he changes the meaning of the term 'justice' in order to claim that the virtue has intrinsic value, redefining it in such terms that its value is obvious, but failing to explain why it is in anyone's interest to be conventionally just in his outward dealings with others.

There is a defence for Socrates against this criticism, based on Book IV (442e–443b), where he claims that someone whose soul is ordered justly, as defined by him, will be highly unlikely to engage in embezzlement, temple robbery, theft, the betrayal of friends or city, adultery, disrespect for parents or neglect of the gods. The suggestion here is that justice in the Socratic sense necessarily *leads* to justice as conventionally conceived. Indeed Socrates argues (443a) that the *cause* of an individual refraining from conventionally unjust action is that 'every part within him does its own work, whether it's ruling or being ruled'. If this is true, then Socrates' defence against the charge of irrelevance is that in recommending his own particular notion of justice as intrinsically valuable, he is effectively recommending a package that contains conventional justice as well, since the former cannot occur without entailing the latter.

The strength of such a defence depends on the plausibility of the claim that Socratic justice typically, or indeed necessarily, results in conventionally just behaviour. We might question this by asking whether it is possible to conceive of an agent who is Socratically just – that is, whose soul is governed by reason, with the other parts subservient – but who is nonetheless conventionally unjust in terms of his outward conduct. Consider a possible character of this kind, whom I shall term a 'rational hedonist'. He is someone who, having rationally deliberated about what sort of life he should lead, determines that personal pleasure is the goal most worth attaining. He thereupon sets about pursuing this end through various conventionally unjust actions: theft, adultery, and so on. Such a person might potentially be described Socratically just insofar as his pattern of conduct issues from reasoning about what it is best for him to do. He is not, in other words, akin to an animal pursuing ends based on the urges of appetite alone. Instead, he coolly and rationally judges that his own pleasure is the most important good, and, having reached this conclusion, does whatever is necessary to attain it.

Plato might respond to this example by denying that the rational hedonist as described above really does manifest Socratic justice. Someone whose life is truly governed by reason, he may argue, would simply *not* come to the conclusion that the life of pleasure was the best. Indeed, such a conclusion is more likely the result of some appetite(s) for pleasure interfering with rational judgement. From Socrates' descriptions of the reasoning part of the soul, he clearly believes this part does not simply motivate an agent to pursue *whatever* end he judges to be good, but also encompasses a specific conception of what 'good' consists in.[40] This is strongly suggested, for example, in Book IX, where reason is characterized as the faculty which 'is always straining to know where the truth lies', and is 'learning-loving and philosophical' (581b–c). It seems from this that someone in whom reason is dominant will choose predominantly intellectual or contemplative goals, rather than sensory pleasure.

If the rational hedonist is not convincing as a case of someone who combines conventional injustice with Socratic justice, we might perhaps wonder about a different type of character, whom I shall term the 'philosophical maniac'. This is someone whose life is so centred around the desire for knowledge that he is willing to engage in all manner of conventionally unjust actions to acquire it. So determined is he, for example, to train at the best university, meet the top academics in his field, build up a comprehensive library and have the free time to focus on learning, that he falsifies documents, bribes college administrators, neglects his familial duties, and steals money to fund his studies. Now, according to Plato's conception of reason as involving a love of knowledge (581b–c), it would seem that reason is very much in charge of this character's soul. Yet he is still, by conventional lights, unjust.

What could Plato say about this case? There is little direct indication from the text. He might perhaps argue that since the life of the philosopher requires few material goods, it is unlikely to involve unjust acts aimed at acquiring them. Socrates, who is often presented by Plato as a rational, truth-seeking paragon, was also noted for his ascetic lifestyle; he required little in material terms to practise his philosophical discussions and therefore had little motivation to cheat or steal. Even if this somewhat romantic picture of the philosopher as beyond material needs is accurate, however, it would not necessarily follow that his conduct would be conventionally just. Justice, in the conventional sense, requires not only that one should refrain from certain harmful acquisitive actions, such as theft, murder, and adultery, but also that one should actively fulfil certain duties, including debt-repayment, respect for one's parents and contribution to social funds. Now, while the 'philosophical maniac' has little reason to engage in the former acts, there surely is a considerable danger that he will disregard the latter in pursuit of the intellectual pursuits his reason-governed soul considers more valuable, thereby sacrificing conventional justice.

For his own part, Plato does not seem to share this concern, as he claims that someone whose soul is justly ordered will respect their parents and duties to the gods (443a). But he offers no explanation of why being governed by reason will lead to fulfilment of these obligations. Moreover, Socrates himself, the supposed paragon of rationality, was so unconcerned for kinship ties that he reputedly sent his wife and child away from his death-bed in order to discuss philosophy with his students.[41] It is unclear, then, how Plato intends to bridge the gap between a soul ruled by reason, conceived in terms of an overriding love of knowledge, and the sorts of active concern for one's responsibilities to others that conventional justice seems to require.

If the link between Socratic and conventional justice is one problem with Plato's account, another involves the relationship between justice in the individual soul and justice in the city. Assuming that the account of the just city is meant not merely as a metaphor for individual justice, but as a serious proposal for political organization, a problem arises about whether members of such a society can also be individually just by Plato's criteria. Such questions can be raised about all three classes in Plato's just state, albeit for different reasons.

In the case of members of the productive class, it is doubtful whether they have sufficient intellectual ability (and training) to stand any chance of becoming rationally-driven, knowledge-oriented individuals. The 'inferior majority' are deemed to manifest 'all kinds of diverse desires, pleasure and pains' (431b–c). This would imply that reason is not predominant in the producers' souls and therefore that, in Socratic terms, they cannot be just. It might be responded that there is a secondary sense in which a producer might attain justice, namely by recognizing that he is incapable of adequately controlling his own passions and that his best option is therefore to live as his rulers, the guardians, prescribe. Whilst, however, this interpretation fits with Plato's pessimistic account of the lower-class members' capabilities, it characterizes the virtue held by producers as involving a very limited use of reason.

The problem of bridging the gap between having a just soul and playing one's role within the just state also arises with respect to the higher castes – the guardians and auxiliaries. The difficulty, in this case, is not with their ability to reason; but rather with the conflict between a rational mindset that wishes above all to pursue learning, and the day-to-day requirements placed on guardians and auxiliaries by their governmental or military duties. Suppose a guardian is individually just: his soul is ruled by reason, and he is thus primarily committed to improving his knowledge. What exactly, we might wonder, will motivate him to carry out his civic role, and ensure that he assigns it sufficient attention and effort, as is required of him by *political* justice? This problem acquires sharper focus later in the *Republic*, when it transpires that guardians, in Plato's view, should be philosophers both by disposition and training. I shall therefore leave further discussion of this question until section 3.9.5.

We have seen that Socrates' account of individual justice raises issues concerning both the answer to Glaucon's challenge, and its interface with the political system he has previously advocated. Book IV ends with Socrates attempting to move on from his definition of justice to categorize various possible unjust states of the soul. But he is interrupted at the start of Book V by a question from Adeimantus, which shifts the focus back onto political matters. The discussion of individual injustice is delayed, consequently, until Book VIII.

Discussion questions:
(a) Plato divides the soul into rational, spirited and appetitive parts. In what other ways have philosophers or psychologists sought to categorize different types of mental or motivational states?

(b) Do you agree that someone governed by their rational part is more likely to behave justly than one dominated by passions and appetites?

3.7. THE JUST STATE – FURTHER DETAILS (449a–474a)

Adeimantus' question is why, in Socrates' initial account of the ideal state, he claimed that wives and children should be held 'in common'? In response, Socrates addresses what he terms three 'waves' of possible criticism of his account of political justice. The first (451c–457c) tackles a somewhat different issue from that which Adeimantus identified, concerning the role of women within the state. The second wave of criticism (457c–461e) deals explicitly with Adeimantus' question about the abolition of the nuclear family. The third wave (beginning 471c) involves the feasibility of the political system Socrates envisages. This section will consider these three areas of discussion in turn. Socrates' response to the third will lead him to introduce one of his most important and controversial proposals, namely the philosopher-ruler, which will be addressed in section 3.8.

3.7.1. The first wave: the status of women

Plato's views about the role of women in Book V have been interpreted by some authors, for instance Gregory Vlastos (1995), as identifying him as a feminist, though others, in particular Julia Annas (1976), strongly repudiate this view. Socrates' argument begins at (451d) with an analogy between the city's guardians and watchdogs. Male dogs, he claims, are mostly stronger and faster than female ones, but females are still eminently capable of guarding and hunting, and it would waste their abilities were they left simply to bear and rear puppies, while males did all the custodial work. In order to use female dogs as guards, however, one must train them the same way as their male counterparts. A similar point applies, Socrates claims, to human 'watch-dogs' – that is, guardians. Although, generally speaking, women are 'weaker' than men, some women are capable of effectively performing governmental duties for the general good of the state, and should therefore be expected to do so. To equip them for the task, moreover, these women require the same training as male guardians, which includes such disciplines as music, poetry, physical training, riding and bearing arms (452b–c).

In defending this argument, Socrates considers a view common in Athenian society but opposed to his own, which denies that women should ever do the same work as men (453b). According to Socrates' account of political justice, everyone must work in accordance with their nature. But, his critics argue, women are by nature very different from men, and therefore should not work in the same spheres, and certainly not that of government. Socrates' response is to dismiss this point as 'quarrelsome and merely verbal' (454b), exploiting a confusion about the word 'nature'. A difference in the 'nature' of two people, he claims, is not always relevant to their respective capabilities for work; bald men are 'different in nature' to long-haired ones (454c), but this does not mean that the former are qualified to be cobblers but not the latter, or indeed vice versa. Similarly, it is only justified to assign different employment to males and females if the differences between the sexes actually affect their abilities to do the relevant jobs. According to Socrates, though, there is no task involved in administering the state that is specific to the attributes of either sex, and indeed there are almost certainly some women who possess the qualities befitting guardians (455d).

Having outlined this seemingly pro-female position, Socrates does add some important reservations. Men are, he says, on average better at all (or nearly all) activities than women, and there are few or no areas of expertise in which females on average outclass males (455c–d). Admittedly, this is *only* 'on average', and it leaves open a possibility that some women, in certain fields, have greater potential than most men do. This is undoubtedly true, for example, of those women who are deemed capable of guardianship. However, since on average men are better in every field, it will probably follow that the most talented of all – those outstanding even *within* the guardian class – will be male. The suggestion that women are never at the apex of any field might, moreover, determine the type of jobs they should be given within government. Socrates argues, for instance, that even though some women may be guardians, 'the lighter parts must be assigned to them because of the weakness of their sex' (457a); they should not be given such important or onerous duties as the elite men.

The main question commentators have asked about Plato's discussion of women's role is to what extent, if any, his proposals are, to use a recent term which he admittedly would not have recognized, 'feminist'. To understand the case for Plato's feminist emancipatory credentials, we first need to look briefly at the status of women in the

Athenian society in which he lived, to see how radical his proposal for female guardians would have appeared. Vlastos[42] offers the following thumbnail sketch of the lives of Athenian women. Those in the middle and upper classes were saddled with domesticity: they seldom went out, were often confined to specific parts of their houses, and had virtually no opportunities for paid employment. Working-class females, by contrast, could engage in a limited number of paid occupations, but these were largely jobs set aside as 'women's work', for instance midwifery and nursing. Women also had little access to public education of either the intellectual or physical varieties, schools and gymnasia being male preserves. Middle and upper class women had scant opportunity for social interaction, and mixed with few men other than their husbands and close relatives. No women were allowed to inherit or own property. And, of course, women had no political rights: they were not eligible to take part in the democratic assemblies, and thus had no input into government. Indeed, they were not regarded as full citizens.

It is obvious that in many ways Socrates' recommendation that some women should be guardians seeks to overturn these social norms. Plato offers his guardian women education in music and poetry, physical training, and other skills necessary for the role. He presents them with opportunities for types of administrative work they would never have had in Athens. Despite the point about them taking on 'lighter' duties, involving them in *any* such occupations would have been a considerable advance. Moreover, Plato assigns guardian women much more freedom to socialize, and, in particular, to socialize with a range of men, than upper-class Athenian women were permitted. It is stated in Book III (416e) that the guardians should live and eat communally, a stipulation which seemingly applies to female guardians as well as males. There is also mention in Book V of the importance of women exercising together with men in gymnasia, despite the embarrassment this may produce due to their being naked (457a–b). Finally, and perhaps most obviously, Plato gives certain women significant *political* power; that is, a role in determining and executing government policy.

If these proposals are the main plank in Vlastos' case for deeming Plato a feminist, the opposing viewpoint is advocated by Annas,[43] who marshals a number of points against his feminist credentials. First, and most simply, she points to his insistence (a) that there is no field in which women's abilities outstrip those of men, and

(b) that, in every area, men are on average more capable than women. Almost all feminists, it seems, would deny (a) and most would probably question (b) too, perhaps maintaining that there are some spheres where women are intrinsically more gifted, such as negotiation, perhaps, or emotional intelligence, or grace of movement. A second point against Plato being a feminist is that whilst his proposals would, if implemented, improve the lives of a small group of elite women, he says little about women in the lower classes, who constitute the majority of society. He does, admittedly, speak several times of women fighting in battle, most explicitly at (466e), and there is the odd passing reference to women being doctors (454d and 455e). On the whole, however, there are few indications that Plato wants to reform policy towards non-guardian women.

The most significant reason, however, for denying that Plato's principles are feminist, on Annas' view[44] concerns his *justification* for the proposal that there should be female guardians. This, she argues, makes no reference whatsoever to the interests or happiness of women themselves in taking such roles, nor indeed to the intrinsic wrongness of denying them rights or opportunities available to men. On the contrary, Plato's main ground for assigning women jobs in government is that it is beneficial to the state to use such female talent as is available. Thus, when concluding his discussion of female guardians, he states that 'the law we've established isn't only possible, it is also optimal *for the city*' (457a, my italics). In response to Annas' point, we might note that whilst it is true that Plato advocates the use of female talent for the civic good rather than that of the talented women, his attitude to male talent is exactly the same. Just as male and female watchdogs are employed alike for their owner's benefit, so both male and female guardians must work to benefit the state, by which they are in some sense owned. Therefore, if Plato's failure to prioritize the happiness of the female guardians means that he is not a feminist, it might be countered that in his treatment of male guardians he is not a masculinist either.

Ultimately, the debate over Plato's feminism is reducible to a disagreement over the meaning of the term. Annas rightly points out that most modern feminists have the interests of women, and, in particular, the wrongness of ignoring these at the heart of their analysis. Plato clearly does not: the starting point of his proposals is the city's overall well-being. On the other hand, if your conditions for labelling a policy 'feminist' depend on the way it actually *treats* women, then Vlastos has a point. He defines feminism in terms of a concern that 'equality in the rights of persons shall not be denied or abridged on account of sex'.[45] In his policy towards the guardians, Plato is not obviously denying or abridging any rights specifically on gender grounds, and indeed his proposals uphold several female rights that contemporary Athens overlooked (though, admittedly, he does not advance these policies *because* of any conception of the rights of individuals). The question of whether this policy counts as feminist, then, depends on whether feminism is thought to hinge on a policy's *content* – the way it actually treats women – or the fundamental moral principles upon which it is based.

3.7.2. The second wave: abolishing the family

The second 'wave' of criticism, to which Socrates turns at (457c), is targeted at his proposal that among the ruling class, wives and children should be held in common; in other words, that there should be no separate nuclear families. The objections levelled at this idea, Socrates notes (458a–b), are likely to concern both the desirability of the arrangements, and the difficulties of instituting them, though in the section (457c–466d) he focuses on the former, shelving the latter for subsequent consideration.

The details of his proposals for sex and childrearing among the guardians, and indeed the auxiliary class, are as follows. He begins by reiterating the point that they should live, eat, and train communally (458c–d), then goes on to suggest that their sexual relations should also be organized by the public authorities. There should be a system of arranged mating rituals (459e), in which guardian (and auxiliary) men and women are brought together to have sex and produce offspring. The government, in selecting who should procreate with whom, should endeavour to conjoin the most able men and women from within their classes, arranging more frequent intercourse for the most talented, as 'a good pretext for them to father as many of the children as possible' (460b). When children are born, the best specimens will be taken into a public rearing pen or crèche, while the lesser offspring will be put to death by exposure (460c). Every effort will be made thereafter to prevent any parents knowing what became of their own children (460d). Moreover, the society will actively discourage any sexual relationship between those of fertile ages outside these state-approved ceremonies, and any child born outside of them will not be supported (461a–b). It will, however, be permitted for older people to have sex with whomsoever they wish, as long as any liaison is guaranteed not to result in incest or pregnancy.

Socrates offers several justifications for these seemingly draconian arrangements. First, he recognizes that some outlet must be provided for sexual urges, but rejects outright promiscuity as impious (458d), and is opposed to marriage and the family for reasons which will become clear. State regulation thus is the least-worst way of organizing sexual intercourse. Secondly, the proposed system is claimed to have eugenic advantages. By breeding from the best men and women, the city will benefit from producing the most talented offspring to become the next generations of guardians and auxiliaries. The underlying assumption is that the qualities required in soldiers and rulers are, to some extent, passed on through heredity.

The third reason for Socrates' scheme, and indeed his main argument for eradicating families among the guardians and auxiliaries, is that it promotes civic unity. In the ideally unified city, 'whenever anything good or bad happens to a single one of its citizens, [the] city will say that the affected part is its own and will share in the pleasure or pain as a whole' (462d–e). In other words, each citizen will identify his or her interests with those of the others. Now, Socrates believes that forbidding separate clans to form among the guardians and auxiliaries will result in every member of these classes treating every other member as one would normally treat one's close relatives. The feelings usually reserved for families are thus extended to a much wider circle, namely the entire class. Each guardian takes pleasure in the successes and well-being of the others, commiserates with their failures or unhappiness, and refrains from any internecine injury. No one considers any fellow member of the class an outsider, as might occur if there were different families among them. The system is thus designed to create a mutually supportive set of rulers, and as Plato claims rather perfunctorily (465b) provided there is no discord among the guardians, 'there's no danger that the rest of the city will break into civil war either' – presumably because it enjoys such an effective ruling force.

Socrates' confidence that abolishing families will result in the widening of the guardians' affections to a larger group is, of course, highly disputable. One might argue on the contrary that it is impossible to have the same strength of concern for the whole of one's social class as one does for the few individuals with whom one has formed private bonds through matrimony or familial life.[46] There is a question, moreover, about the exact psychological mechanism through which Socrates believes this extension of feeling will take place. At one stage (463c) he suggests that the reason why every guardian under his scheme treats every other as a blood relation is that, as far as he or she knows, any one of them might *actually* be. Since no one's parentage is divulged by the state, it is possible that anyone of an appropriate age group could be one's parent, sibling, child or other close relative. Hence, if one were to harm a fellow guardian, it is possible that one might thereby damage one's own blood-line. Somewhat paradoxically, then, it seems Socrates relies on the biological urge to nurture one's family to motivate concern for fellow guardians in a society where no families exist.

A theme running throughout the political sections of the *Republic*, which resurfaces in the passage on sex and childrearing, is Plato's willingness to use individuals of any class as means to promoting the greater good of the entire state, even where this seemingly involves a considerable sacrifice of their individual happiness. The guardians are to be denied private relationships, it appears, primarily because this makes theirs a more efficient and unified government, which is beneficial to the state as a whole. Socrates admits that his chief concern is with the city's happiness rather than that of any particular individual, though he does add that guardians living under his arrangements should not be terribly unhappy, as they will benefit from their freedom from what he deems 'ignoble' concerns about private and household finances (466a–c). They will also, he says, be supported by public funds in the manner of Olympian victors (465d); therefore any guardian who complains about his or her treatment is guilty of immoderate 'adolescent' demands (466b–c) and has the wrong conception of happiness. Socrates may thus deny the charge that his system severely exploits the ruling class *en masse*, though there will surely still be some individuals whose interests are significantly compromised for the greater good, such as the less talented guardians who are afforded few chances to procreate, and indeed the unfortunate infants who are summarily put to death.

3.7.3. The third wave: an unachievable ideal?

At (471c), we reach the third and perhaps most fundamental 'wave' of objection to Socrates' state, which concerns the practicality of the ideal system he has outlined. Glaucon asks, even if we accept that Socrates' proposals have all the advantages and virtues he describes, is it possible that such a system could actually come into being, or is it simply an unattainable ideal?

Socrates' initial response (472b–e) is to say that even if the ideal cannot be achieved, it is worth talking about *as* an ideal by philosophers; just as it is a valid project for a painter to try to depict the most beautiful human being possible, even if such a person could never exist. Presumably, in addition to being of purely theoretical interest, such an ideal might serve as a measure for the justice of existing states, which depends upon how far they resemble the perfect one. Socrates also argues, however, that the state he outlines is not completely unobtainable; indeed, he will show 'how and under what conditions it would most be possible to found such a city' (472e). He then proceeds to drop a bombshell: the necessary condition for achieving the ideal constitution is that 'political power and philosophy entirely coincide' (473c). The just state will not be attained 'until philosophers rule as kings in cities or those who are now called kings and leading men genuinely and adequately philosophise . . .' (ibid.). This is a significant development in Socrates' account of the guardians; for the first time we are told that they must be, or at least become, philosophers. The suggestion is received with amazement by Glaucon, who orders Socrates to justify himself or else face 'general derision' (474a). Socrates' response is that he needs to explain what he means by a philosopher before he can adequately defend his proposal. I will next examine his sketch of the philosopher ruler, and assess his reasons for believing such a person is most likely to offer good government.

Discussion questions:

(a) In various passages of the *Republic*, Socrates makes blatantly misogynist remarks. How do these square with his relatively positive portrayal of female ability and potential in Book V?[47]

(b) What effects would the abolition of the family unit, together with arrangements to prevent people knowing the identity of their close relatives, have on interpersonal relationships within a community?

3.8. THE PHILOSOPHER RULER (474b–504a)

The first hint of justification for the view that philosophers should rule in the ideal state is offered at (474b–c). Those who are 'fitted by nature' for philosophy, it is claimed, are also suitable for jobs in government. The end of Book V and the beginning of Book VI are devoted to explaining what it is about philosophers that fits them for the task of ruling. The reasons, in essence, are twofold. First, according to Plato, only trained philosophers possess the *knowledge* necessary to govern well; and second, he believes their moral and intellectual virtues to be superior to those of others. This commentary will address these two points in turn, whilst also considering several objections to Socrates' defence of the philosopher-ruler thesis, and analysing Plato's attempts to counter the charge that his proposal for a 'philosophical' government runs contrary to common sense.

3.8.1. Knowledge and the Forms

Philosophers are typified, Socrates claims, by their desire for 'all kinds' of wisdom and learning (475c); they do not restrict their pursuit of knowledge to any particular area. Glaucon objects (475d) that there are many people who desire a wide range of knowledge who are surely not philosophers – those, for instance, who enjoy attending festivals and plays, or spend their time learning a vast array of 'petty crafts'. Socrates admits that these 'lovers of sights and sounds' are not philosophers, though their desire for knowledge does make them somewhat similar (475e). They lack the genuine philosophical nature, however, because there is an important area of learning they do *not* pursue, namely learning about ideas – the essential nature of phenomena such as beauty, justice, goodness, knowledge, and so forth. In other words, while they are eager to know about *particular* objects which possess properties of these kinds – for instance, particular beautiful sights or sounds – they are not disposed to investigate what beauty itself (for example) consists in (see 476b).

It is essential at this point to introduce one of the most controversial notions in Plato's philosophy, which appears in the *Republic* at (476a), namely that of Forms (or Ideas; the terms for our purposes are interchangeable). There exist, on a Platonic view, certain objects which possess properties – beauty, justice, goodness, etc. – in unqualified ways. The Form of beauty is unqualifiedly beautiful, the

Form of justice unqualifiedly just, the Form of goodness is perfectly good, and so on. When philosophers investigate the nature of beauty, justice, or any such property, their project is effectively to analyse the corresponding Form; that is, the nature of the object which possesses this property in unconditional terms. Particular physical objects, by contrast – trees, flowers, tables, people, etc. – may possess these properties to certain degrees, but never without qualification: no flower is unqualifiedly beautiful, or no person unqualifiedly just, for reasons that will be outlined presently.

There are several suggestions in the *Republic* (476a–d) as to how Forms and Particulars interrelate. At (476a), it is said that Forms 'manifest themselves [. . .] in association' with Particulars; at (476c), Particulars are *likenesses* of Forms; and at (476d) particular objects *participate* in the Forms corresponding to their properties. So, for example, a particular beautiful flower might be said either to accompany a manifestation of the Form of beauty, to be a likeness of this Form, or to participate in it. It is debatable, at a textual level, whether Plato adheres to a consistent view of the relationship between Form and Particulars. A more pressing question, however, is how Forms relate to the claim that philosophers are best fitted to govern the city. The last part of Book V comprises two arguments whose purpose is to show that only philosophers, who study the Forms, truly gain knowledge (*epistemē*). By contrast, practical people or 'lovers of sights and sounds', who seek to learn about particular objects, acquire only opinion or belief (*doxa*). As Plato goes on to claim, the knowledge possessed by philosophers can be put to good use in the business of government. These arguments, then, constitute a significant plank in his case in favour of the philosopher-ruler.

The first of them (476b–d) refers specifically to the notion of Forms, and trades on a contrast between the philosopher – someone who knows about these objects – and the worldly individual, who may have plenty to say about particular beautiful scenes, good people, etc., but who has no knowledge of the Forms of beauty and goodness, and maybe does not even recognize their existence (476b). Moreover, the lover of particular things even mistakes Particulars for Forms possessing similar properties; as Socrates puts it, he is given to thinking 'that a likeness [a Particular] is not a likeness but rather the thing itself that it is like [a Form]' (476c). This last charge seems rather odd, for if lovers of sights and sounds do not believe that Forms exist (as Socrates claims) it is curious that they should mistake particular objects for them. Furthermore, identifying a Particular as a Form is simply a bizarre kind of error to make. There is admittedly a plausible, albeit weaker, point that there is an important *area* of knowledge which lovers of sights and sounds lack, namely knowledge of Forms. But granted this, we might well ask why knowledge of Forms is more important than knowledge of Particulars when it comes to the qualifications for governing a city.

Socrates' response to this question is a radical one, found in his next, somewhat lengthy argument, at the end of Book V (476e–480). This argument is specifically addressed to students of Particulars who believe, incorrectly in Socrates' view, that they have knowledge of a sort to rival that of philosophers. It is intended to convince them that, on the contrary, they possess no knowledge at all. The point of this argument is that the *only* things about which knowledge can be acquired are the Forms: the abstract objects analysed by philosophy. By contrast, particular sights and sounds, and the everyday physical objects associated with them, cannot be objects of knowledge, but only of opinion (*doxa*). Hence, those who study them, but ignore the Forms, lack knowledge altogether, and are consequently unsuitable for appointment as guardians.

Socrates' argument for the view that knowledge attaches to Forms and not Particulars begins with his stating a rather contentious principle to the effect that knowledge and opinion are different powers (*dunameis*) with mutually exclusive sets of objects (478a–b). Things which are objects of knowledge cannot be objects of opinion, and vice versa. This principle conflicts with the commonsense view that the same things may be objects of knowledge, held by some people, and opinions, held by others: for example, while you might hold the opinion that I am over thirty years old, I know this to be true. The principle is not strictly necessary, however, for Socrates' main line of argument, which is based on the following four premises, scattered throughout the section (477–479):

(a) (477a): knowledge is about *what is.*
(b) (477b): opinion is about *what is intermediate between what is and what is not.*
(c) (Argued at 479a–d): particular objects, such as beautiful sights and sounds, are *intermediates between what is and what is not*; or *intermediate between being and not being.*

(d) (Implied at 479e): Forms (the objects philosophers study) are instances of *what is* absolutely.

Now, if one accepts all four of these points, then it follows from (a) and (d) that knowledge is about Forms (i.e. Forms are objects of knowledge), and from (b) and (c) that opinion is about Particulars. This argument is complex, and there is a great deal of scholarly disagreement over its interpretation, much of which is beyond the scope of this commentary. Most of the argument centres on how we should understand the phrases, italicized above, involving the terms *what is* and *what is not*. Cross and Woozley[48] take *what is* to mean *what exists*, and *what is not* to mean *what does not exist*. This interpretation has its problems, however, as it suggests that there are degrees of existence, with some objects (namely Particulars) being intermediate between existing and not existing. It is not altogether clear what this would mean, though there are admittedly suggestions elsewhere in the *Republic* that Plato holds particular objects to be less 'real' than Forms. At (476c), for instance, Particulars are said to be mere 'likenesses' of Forms, and in Book X (597c–d) it is claimed that the 'truly real bed' is not the type that a carpenter makes, but rather the Form of Bed. The interpretation also has other pitfalls. Regarding point (b), for instance, it would seem strange to claim that we only hold opinions about things that are, in Plato's sense, part way between existing and not existing. Where does this leave opinions about things which definitely do not exist at all – for instance, an opinion about a character in a fictional novel?

Annas[49] offers a different interpretation of the argument, which takes *what is* to mean *what is F*, or in other words *what has a certain property F*, where F could for example be beauty, justice, largeness or redness. On Annas' reading, point (a) states that one can only know something to have a property, for instance beauty, if it actually has that property. Next, (b) says that the circumstances where one might hold the opinion that an object is, say, beautiful, are where it is part way between being beautiful and not being so; in other words, where its beauty is somehow partial, relative, conditional or limited. Then, point (c) reads that particular objects are essentially intermediate between the possession and non-possession of qualities such as beauty; and point (d) that Forms possess these properties in unconditional ways. Thus, one cannot have knowledge that a Particular is (say) beautiful, because no particular object is actually beautiful in an unqualified sense. One can have such knowledge, however, about the Form of beauty. The same applies to other properties: one can know that they belong to Forms, but only have opinions about particular objects possessing them.

The biggest question about the argument, thus interpreted, is how Socrates seeks to justify point (c): the claim that a particular object can only ever be intermediate between the possession and non-possession of a given property. His justification for this is given at (479a–b), where he asks whether 'of all the many beautiful things, is there one that will not also appear ugly? Or is there one of those just things that will not also appear unjust?' Equally, he goes on, doubles can appear to be halves, big objects can appear small, and light ones heavy. In short, as Glaucon puts it, a particular object 'always participates in both opposites' (479b). In Annas' terms, this means for any Particular that can be described as having a given property F, it is also possible to describe it, under certain conditions, as lacking this property. Thus, it is *intermediate between being and not being F.*

The examples chosen by Socrates to make this point appear to have been quite carefully selected. Some of them involve properties which are relational; that is, whose ascription to one object is only meaningful in relation to another. Take the property 'double'. It makes little sense simply to say 'four is double', unless we relate this number to another: 'four is double two'. Similarly, 'Athens is large' is a somewhat empty statement unless we compare its size with something else; it is large in relation to a village but not in relation to planet Earth. Socrates' claim, then, that such Particulars 'participate in both opposites', in these cases at least, may be taken to mean that they can be assigned opposing properties depending on which objects they are compared with.

The properties of beauty and justice, which Socrates also uses as examples, are not relational in the same sense; their ascription to an object can be meaningful without relating it to another. However, their ascription might still be conditional on certain factors. Arguably, in the case of beauty, whether or not something is beautiful depends on who is making the assessment. Its beauty may also depend on the time at which it is assessed: the same city may be beautiful at one point in time, but not 50 years later when it has become industrialized. Regarding justice, the just nature of a particular type of action may depend on the precise circumstances in which it is performed. Recall Socrates' debate with Cephalus in

Book I. The latter said that giving back what you have borrowed is just, and Socrates replied that this is not the case if a known lunatic has lent you his weapon. Thus, the action of 'giving back what you borrow' is just under certain conditions, but unjust under others. Again, one might therefore say that it both has and does not have the property of justice.

The crux of the argument, thus interpreted, is that it is impossible to know that a Particular has a given property, because it cannot have this property in an unconditional sense. Rather, its having the property depends, if not on relating it to another object, then on the fulfilment of some contingent condition(s). If this is supposed to show that one can never have knowledge about Particulars, however, it is open to strong objections. First, while the properties Socrates has chosen to list are, indeed, ones whose ascription is always conditional, there are other properties where this is not the case. Annas[50] raises the example of 'being a man' – let us perhaps rather say 'being male' to avoid any disagreement about the age when one achieves manhood. It is hard to see how Socrates, for example, could be said both to *be and not be* male; surely he unconditionally *is*, and therefore from point (a) it is possible to *know* this fact. Secondly, the move from denying that Particulars can have properties unconditionally to saying that one cannot know about the properties they possess is rather suspect. Why, it might be countered, can someone not have knowledge that certain objects are beautiful, just, large and so forth, *in conditional ways*? Why, for example, can you not know that Athens is large compared to a village, or that the majority of people who visit the city today find it beautiful, or that repaying your kindly old mother the money she lent you is a just action?

It is not clear how Plato would answer these points. Perhaps, in response to the second, he would claim that non-philosophers – lovers of sights and sounds – often fail to recognize the conditions under which certain properties are accurately ascribed, and consequently assent to sweeping, and therefore either meaningless or misleading, statements of the kind: 'Athens is large', 'my house is beautiful', 'repaying debts is just'. In other words, they lack knowledge about these Particulars, because they ascribe them properties unconditionally, which they in fact possess only in conditional ways. It would still seem an overstatement on Plato's part, however, to insist that everyone who lacks a philosophical training, and is concerned with Particulars rather than Forms, is guaranteed to make this type of error. On the contrary, it seems perfectly feasible that someone should, for instance, recognize that the same object is beautiful to some people but not to others, or beautiful only at certain times of its existence, without having studied philosophical aesthetics or being able to give an account of the nature of beauty itself.

Despite these doubts over Plato's claim that knowledge acquisition is limited to philosophers, he does, in Book VI, offer an interesting account of how philosophers might use their special knowledge of Forms to help govern a city. This begins with the argument that those who do not know the Forms have 'no clear model in their souls of what is most true' and hence cannot establish 'conventions about what is fine or just or good' (484c–d). This implies that in order to build civic laws and institutions that are as far as possible fine, good, or just, one must first understand what the undiluted qualities of fineness, justice and goodness consist in – facts which are known only to philosophers. A similar point appears at (500d–501c): a philosopher ruler can examine the Forms, and seek to 'put what he sees into people's characters, whether into a single person or into a populace', making him 'a good craftsman of moderation, justice, and the whole of virtue'. Again, the suggestion is that government is best conducted by someone who knows, in theory, what these virtues are, and can thus devise political policies to inculcate them in society. The most important Form to be used in the business of government is the Form of the Good: as Socrates claims at (505e), 'everyone pursues the good', but most people do not know what goodness is. Only philosophers can acquire this knowledge, so the guardians' education should focus on giving them the philosophical techniques to gain a true account of the nature of goodness itself.

3.8.2. The philosopher's character

Philosophers' knowledge of Forms provides them with a theoretical basis for government. Their understanding of what it is to be good and virtuous renders them best placed to imbue these qualities in a city. But such knowledge is not enough. Socrates stipulates that philosophers should only govern provided they are not inferior to other citizens 'either in experience or in any other part of virtue' (484d). He goes on, however, to claim that philosophers are likely to be superior to others in terms of both moral and intellectual qualities. A philosopher is marked out, in contrast to 'honour lovers' and 'erotically inclined men', by a love of *truth* (485b–c); moreover he desires pleasures of the soul in preference to those of the body (485d). Consequently, he is generally uninterested in activities requiring large amounts of money. Equally, as a student of 'all time and all being' he will not consider one human life – even his own – to be of great importance, hence he will have little fear of death. There are definite overtones of Socrates himself in this description of the philosophical character; in particular his overriding desire for knowledge, his disdain for material goods, and his courage regarding his own mortality.

Plato wants to claim that a philosopher's idiosyncratic mindset makes him potentially a 'reliable and just' ruler (486b). He does not offer specific arguments to this effect, but it is possible to extrapolate several reasons. For instance, a philosopher will waste less time on the pursuit of pleasure, money, or trivialities than other men; indeed, it is said that 'pettiness' is incompatible with a philosophical nature (486a). He is also less likely to be corruptible than someone who desires worldly goods. Since he is indifferent to these things he cannot be bribed or seduced into neglecting his duties, nor will he be tempted to abuse his position in pursuit of such goals. We can suppose, furthermore, that his love of truth makes him averse to carrying out deceptive or duplicitous actions whilst in office. Finally, since he is unconcerned with his own death, he is likely to be unusually self-sacrificing for the good of the city.

In addition to a philosopher's special knowledge of Forms and his ethical character, a third factor making him a good ruler (486c–487a) is the *intellectual* ability associated with his skill in philosophy. To be a good philosopher, one must be a quick learner, have a good memory and 'measured and graceful' (486d) thought processes. A person who possesses such qualities, however, will also be able to govern the state effectively. Thus, the same attributes that produce success and interest in philosophy are also welcome in a guardian.

3.8.3. Democracy versus rule by experts

Plato is aware that his proposal for philosopher-rulers is highly controversial. He demonstrates this by having Adeimantus object (487a–d) that while Socrates' manner of argument is characteristically persuasive, his conclusion that philosophers should rule seems downright implausible. Common sense, by contrast, says that the majority of those who spend their time on philosophy become 'cranks, not to say completely vicious' (487d), while the rest are rendered 'useless to the city' (ibid.) by their chosen studies.

Socrates' response to this objection is subtle and indirect, requiring a considerable amount of interpretation. He begins with an extended metaphor, the 'Ship of State' (488a–e). We are asked to imagine a ship, whose owner is physically strong, but hard of hearing and short-sighted, and knows little or nothing about seafaring. Various sailors on board the ship, who are equally deficient in the art of navigation and indeed believe that no particular skill is necessary to sail well, all wish to control the rudder; each making every attempt to persuade the ship-owner to assign him this responsibility. These men squabble for power, and even attempt to drug the ship-owner so that they can take over without his consent. Moreover, they regard whoever is successful in getting control of the ship, either by persuasion or force, as being a true navigator and captain; in other words, they think that it is the ability to attain power, rather than any skill at seafaring itself, which warrants such accolades. They also dismiss anyone who is really capable of sailing the ship well, but who refuses to become involved in their struggles for power, as being a mere 'stargazer' (488e) and good-for-nothing.

The metaphor is seemingly for a democratic system of government, like that of ancient Athens. The ship represents the city, and navigation the art of government. The mass of sailors are 'those who rule in existing cities' (489c); and the ignorant ship-owner, who is empowered to select which of them rules, is the general public, which chooses its officials but lacks any knowledge of how the city should be run. The sailors' efforts to persuade the ship-owner to put them in charge represent the strivings of demagogues in a democracy, who, despite their ignorance of government, grapple for power and seek to trick the public into granting them a mandate. Like the sailors, such politicians' skills and interests revolve around achieving power within the current system, and indeed they deny that there is anything to ruling besides the ability to attain a position by flattering or deceiving the electorate.

Correspondingly, the person who *really* knows what is good for the state – in Socrates' view, the philosopher – is, like the captain in the metaphor, dismissed as a useless theoretician. As he refuses to become embroiled in entreating the public (the ship-owner) for power, not only is his expert knowledge wasted, but he is not even recognized as a good politician, for he is too detached from the system to engage in the necessary self-promotion. The metaphor, therefore, serves two purposes. It presents a strong critique of democracy, claiming that the system denies a city government by those best suited to the task (i.e. philosophers), instead promoting ignorant and egotistical career-politicians. But equally, it attempts to explain why philosophers are not highly regarded within the system as it stands.

Opponents of Socrates' proposal for philosophical rule fall into two broad camps. First, there are those who may agree with the thrust of the criticism of democracy implied by the Ship of State metaphor – believing that government should be conducted by knowledgeable experts – but who dispute Socrates' more specific claim that the experts in question are philosophers. This group might question the assumption, implicit in Socrates' account of how philosopher-rulers govern, that studying philosophy results in the discovery of objective truths about what is good, of a kind which can be used as an unequivocal platform for policy-making. The history of disagreement among renowned ethicists would suggest that, even assuming there *are* such things as facts about what is ultimately valuable (itself a highly questionable claim), philosophical investigation has not produced a clear and indisputable account of what they are. Socrates' government by philosophers, then, seems at best likely to be characterized by considerable internal disagreement.

Moreover, even if we grant that philosophy can discover the nature of virtue and goodness, and that such knowledge can be successfully brought to bear on political practice, it might still be true that other aspects of government require different types of expertise. For example, one might doubt whether a philosophical training alone is sufficient to produce experts in the details of economic policy, administration of funds, or diplomatic relations with other states. These areas at least, it would seem, require people with a more practical training to work alongside philosophers.

Socrates' second group of opponents are those who favour democratic methods of decision-making over elitist ones. Again, this group has several arguments at its disposal, two of which I shall consider, borrowing examples from Ross Harrison (1993). The first is that in some cases of public decision-making, there is simply no kind of expertise which is helpful in making the best decision. Harrison's example[51] is of a group of people deciding the colour of a uniform for the group as a whole to wear, where no questions of visibility, camouflage, or cost or availability of different coloured materials are at stake. In this scenario, there is no expert, or group of experts, who are most likely to choose the 'right' colour, for there is no sense in which any colour *is* the right one, except in that it satisfies the wishes of the (majority of the) group. Thus, there is no apparent reason to oppose a democratic method of making this decision. Since it is simply a matter of aggregating the preferences of those concerned, finding out what the majority want and choosing it seems the best course.

Admittedly the majority of political decisions are not of this kind, but rather fall under the sphere of some kind of expertise, be it economic, sociological, diplomatic, military or even ethical. However, it does not follow from the fact that some expertise is relevant to a political decision that the best option to take is necessarily that which reflects the 'expert' view. Harrison uses the following, military example:[52] a group is under attack and needs to determine which of two geographical positions to defend. One of them, position A, is the more easily defensible given the nature of the terrain, the group's strengths and weaknesses and those of its enemy. The expert soldiers among the group, moreover, are able to identify this fact. However, for some reason, the vast majority of the group, who have little knowledge of warfare, prefer the other position, B, and their preference is so strong that they would be very unwilling to defend position A if it were chosen. Indeed, the loss in morale that would result from the group choosing position A would be so great that their defeat would be more likely than if position B were chosen, notwithstanding the intrinsic advantages of the former position.

The point of this is that it may be more important, when determining public policy, to choose options that are widely *believed* to be right, than to attain the benefits of following expert knowledge. If experts are left to decide and public opinion is not accounted for, then the negative effects of the majority disagreeing with the chosen policy may even be so great as to outweigh the advantages of the choice being made by the better-informed minority. It may be better, therefore, to decide the policy democratically, thus ensuring a course that the majority will support, and willingly put into practice. A modern day example might be the UK's decision over whether to participate in the Single European Currency. Even if all financial experts agreed that joining was in Britain's interests, it might be argued that the loss of national morale which would result from doing so without public consent might more than counterbalance its economic benefits.

This argument would no doubt have cut little ice with Plato, as we recall that in his picture of the ideal city, the auxiliaries and producers willingly accept their rule by the guardians (431d–e). Reluctance to accept the rulers' decisions would specifically imply a lack of political 'moderation' and should therefore be discouraged, though how this is to be prevented, other than by totalitarian means, is a moot point.

3.8.4. Public perceptions of philosophy: the three 'types' of philosopher

I shall now return to Socrates' response to Adeimantus' speech at (487a–d). Adeimantus, as previously outlined, draws attention to philosophers' poor reputation in contemporary society. The majority of them, he says, are regarded as vicious cranks, with the remainder viewed as somewhat useless individuals, at least politically. Socrates' reply to this point combines further justification for the proposal that philosophers should govern, with a thinly veiled defence, on Plato's part, of Socrates himself, against the charges which eventually led to his execution.

Socrates surprisingly begins his response by agreeing with those who condemn present-day philosophers as either dangerous or practically ineffectual (487d). But he is careful to qualify this by saying that these allegations are true of those who *profess* to engage in philosophy (489c–d). In the following passage (490–497), he distinguishes three different types of so-called 'philosophical' character. The first are people who have a 'philosophic nature' (490c) but who are corrupted by society and therefore fail to pursue philosophy in a serious way. By 'philosophic nature', Socrates means the intellectual and moral attributes making one suitable for philosophical study; for example 'courage, high-mindedness, ease in learning, and a good memory' (ibid.). Paradoxically, in Socrates' view, people who possess these properties are likely to be drawn, by various forces in society, away from philosophical study. The most naturally gifted may be encouraged by their families and fellow-citizens to seek leading positions within their city. However, given the Athenian democratic system, in order to be successful in politics one must adapt oneself to reflect, in various respects, the opinions of the general public (492b–d).

Socrates develops his account of how politicians operate in democracies with a metaphor: their task is like that of 'learning the moods and appetites of a huge, strong, beast' (493b). The democratic politician is limited to governing in the way most likely to keep this beast, i.e. the general public, happy. Moreover, he loses any sense of the value of policies aside from their popularity; in Socrates' words, he calls 'what [the beast] enjoys good and what angers it bad' (493c). He is forced, in other words, to assess the merits of political ideas and actions solely with reference to public opinion. We are familiar with this type of approach to politics from the role of focus-groups and opinion polls in our own society. The danger with these, from a Platonic perspective, is that, in seeking to establish the worth of different policies, they focus only on considerations of what will get the most votes, not what is really in society's best interests.

The corruption of political leaders in a democracy is not restricted, moreover, to their choosing crowd-pleasing policies. In order to succeed in the system, they have to 'follow the same way of life' and 'be the same sort of people' as the majority (492c), otherwise they will be offputting to the electorate. Again, this has echoes in democracies of today, with the efforts made by many politicians to come across as 'ordinary' people to whom the public can relate. Whatever one's opinion of such practices, they are clearly anathema to Plato, who takes a dim view of the character of the uneducated masses and deems it the duty of government to control their desires and impose lawfulness on their behaviour (431c–d). Guardians should be of a superior stamp, making them worthy to govern their inferiors. In a democracy, however, political leaders must be like the people they govern, and this discourages them from studying philosophy, a subject 'inevitably disapproved of' (494a) by the majority, who do not understand it. Thus, the most able youngsters in the city, earmarked for political careers, are forced by the public or their patrons to focus on practical politics to the exclusion of ethical theory, thereby losing sight of the very ideals on which their practice should be based. Their corruption is further compounded by the flattery of the masses, which is liable to make them conceited (494c–d).

The story of the talented youth being drafted into a senior political role and thereby corrupted is part of Plato's extended critique of his own society, and of democracy in general. It may also have a more specific reference, however, to Alcibiades, a colourful character in Athenian history, who was in his youth a friend and associate of Socrates. Indeed, there were widespread rumours of a sexual relationship between the two, though Plato himself, in the *Symposium*, seems to deny that Socrates had any such interest. Alcibiades became an extremely popular politician and general, whose intelligence, good looks and ability to play to an audience won him many supporters. In 415 BC, however, he was accused of taking part in a serious act of vandalism: a number of public statues of the god Hermes had been mutilated, and Alcibiades was thought to have participated in this, possibly as a protest against Athenian military policy. He was recalled from duty in Sicily, but rather than facing his accusers he fled to Sparta, a major enemy of Athens, and advised the Spartan leadership on how they could defeat his mother city. Later, he had disagreements with the Spartans too, and re-established himself with a group of Athenian officers opposed to the democratic system, helping them in 411 BC to plot a (short-lived) oligarchic coup to take over Athens.

Judging from Alcibiades' chequered career, it seems that he was someone who possessed the sorts of virtues that, in Socrates' view, characterize the 'philosophical nature'; but who was spoiled by his engagement in practical politics, and underwent a moral decline which eventually led to treason. One of Plato's purposes in having Socrates tell a similar story in Book VI may be to repudiate one of the charges on which Socrates himself was indicted, namely that of corrupting the Athenian youth. Socrates' friendship with Alcibiades – a notorious figure in Athenian history – was perhaps one of the reasons he acquired this reputation. In this passage in Book VI however, Plato seeks to deny that Socrates, and his brand of philosophical teaching, were responsible for Alcibiades' corruption. Instead, he lays this charge at the door of Athenian democracy: it was the young man's involvement in this system, and his flattery by the general public, that made him over-ambitious, petulant, and too concerned with status, meaning that when his reputation was questioned he left the city to join its enemies.

The result of the most talented individuals eschewing philosophy is that the discipline is taken over by another group. These are the second type of 'philosopher' alluded to: pseudo-philosophers (495c–e) who lack the qualities required to do the subject well, but who nonetheless attempt to fill the vacancy left by the more able.

Socrates is particularly scathing about this group of second-raters, 'bald-headed tinkers' (496e) whom he believes largely responsible for philosophers' general reputation as vicious cranks. There is little explicit detail given about the type of 'philosophy' engaged in by these individuals, but from various references in Book VI and elsewhere we can build a picture of the sorts of contemporary philosophical practices Socrates so despised. At (496a), he attacks the propagation of 'sophisms, things that have nothing genuine about them or worthy of being called true wisdom'. Later (499a) he contrasts the 'sophistications and eristic quibbles' common among the Athenian intelligentsia with what a true philosopher would provide, namely 'fine and free arguments that search out the truth in every way for the sake of knowledge'.

The term *eristic* is important here. It means, broadly speaking, argument or debate for the sake of victory over one's opponents, as opposed to *dialectic*, discussion aimed at finding out the truth. The main complaint levelled at contemporary Sophists – the professional philosophers operating in Athens – is that they 'aim at nothing except reputation and disputation' (ibid.). They are more concerned with showing off verbal and argumentative skills than with the pursuit of truth and knowledge. Moreover, their brand of philosophy may be dangerous, especially when used, as it often was, to undermine social mores. Later, in Book VII (537e–539d), Socrates describes how young people, exposed to clever sophistic refutations of the conventional moral precepts they were taught in childhood, are encouraged to become sceptical and 'lawless', rejecting the sound advice of their elders.

There is, again, an element of defence of Socrates himself intertwined with this attack on Athenian sophistry. The playwright Aristophanes' work *The Clouds* depicted philosophers as clever wordsmiths who sought to undermine morality; as he put it, to make the 'wrong' argument defeat the 'right'. *The Clouds* tells of an unscrupulous man who studies philosophy because he wants to avoid paying his debts, and believes the subject will furnish him with the skills to argue his way out of financial obligations. The person who teaches him to do so, moreover, is none other than a caricatured version of Socrates himself. Now, Plato clearly wishes to deny that Socrates would engage in such practices, so he has Socrates himself suggest that they were in fact the work of 'philosophers' hardly worthy of the name – second-rate professionals who lack the true philosopher's (and by implication, his own) love of truth, and who rather view the subject, at best, as a word-game and at worst as a means of encouraging moral scepticism. These people cannot, however, practice philosophy in the right way, since they lack the ability; the only reason they have the opportunity to ply their trade at all is that their superiors have vacated the field to pursue political careers.

There is, however, a small third group, comprising those who both have the qualities needed to philosophize, and who manage to avoid being drawn away from the subject (496a–e). These are the people who would, in Plato's view, be suitable for government, but they are also the group which is generally regarded as practically useless. The reasons for their perceived uselessness are twofold. First, once these philosophers have experienced the pleasures of the intellectual life, they are unlikely to want to enter the public arena, a sphere in which 'hardly anyone acts sanely' (496c). Second, even if they did seek political careers, they would have difficulty making any impact given the way politics is presently conducted. This is implied when Socrates compares the philosopher in political life to one who has fallen among wild animals, and is 'neither willing to join them in doing injustice nor sufficiently strong to oppose the general savagery alone' (496d). Part of the reason for the philosopher's inability to deal with the political world is precisely that he operates on a higher intellectual level, using abstract concepts of which the majority are ignorant. In Book VII, Socrates describes a philosopher in court, who appears ridiculous when seeking 'to dispute about the way things are understood by people who have never seen justice itself' (517e). This seems, again, a veiled reference to Socrates' own trial, and a justification of his failure to convince the jury of his innocence. More generally, the picture of the 'true' philosopher as neither willing, nor especially able, to contribute to public affairs under the current system is a reflection of Socrates' own preference for staying out of politics.

On the other hand, Plato clearly believes that philosophers have the potential to govern a city better than anyone else. This depends, however, on their being able to operate within the right sort of political framework, in particular being free from the democratic constraint of having to appeal to the majority. Again, in the 'Ship of State' metaphor, the 'true' captain who knows best how to navigate fails to do so, both because he refuses to jockey for position with the other sailors, and because he would not be successful at gaining power amongst such individuals. The fault, however, is not with the captain (or the philosopher), but rather with the system which does not allow their abilities to be utilized. Plato therefore calls for a constitutional overhaul, in which public policy is refocused on educating the most naturally gifted in philosophical thought, and placing power in their hands alone. Under such conditions, 'the philosopher's own growth will be fuller, and he'll save the community as well as himself' (497a).

3.8.5. Instituting philosophical government

There remain questions of whether societies could ever be convinced that the system of philosopher-rulers would work, and whether such a system could really be instituted. To 'sell' the philosopher-ruler thesis it is important to spell out clearly what one means by a true philosopher (see 499e): that is, a rational and virtuous intellectual dedicated to, and able to attain, knowledge of the Forms. Unfortunately, the political status-quo involves a vicious circle. Socrates' ideally just state, he admits in Book V, cannot come about until philosophers take over government (473d–e). However, given the present political system (an unjust one, in Socrates' eyes), it is highly unlikely that philosophers will come to govern. It seems, then, that political justice cannot be achieved until philosophers rule, and that equally, until there are just institutions, the advent of philosopher-rulers is improbable.

The only way to break the cycle, Socrates claims, is through some 'chance event', involving either the few 'true' philosophers in a city entering government, or the current rulers being divinely inspired to embrace philosophy (499b). These events, though unlikely, are not impossible over the entire course of history (499c–d). Moreover, once philosophers have the chance to govern a state, and effect appropriate changes in its constitution, Socrates is convinced that the citizens will acknowledge the merits of these changes and gladly obey the new laws (502b). In other words, once people witness philosophical rule in action, they will accept it as being in the city's best interests. The constitutional alterations introduced by philosophers, moreover, will ensure that the study of philosophy is made compulsory for all future guardians. Thus, once initiated, the system will perpetuate itself, and the city will reap the many benefits that knowledge of the Forms, and the other virtues of a philosophical nature, can bring.

Discussion questions:
(a) Is the main purpose of philosophy the pursuit of knowledge? What other functions might the discipline have?
(b) Does the case for democracy break down if some people are shown to be better than others at political decision-making?
(c) Are Adeimantus' remarks about the commonplace distrust and suspicion of philosophers applicable to today's society? If so, how would you account for this phenomenon?

3.9. THE SUN, THE LINE AND THE CAVE (504b–541b)

In order to build and maintain a society which is just and virtuous, philosopher-rulers must understand the character of justice and the other virtues. For Plato, as we have seen, this requires their having studied the relevant Forms, especially the Form of the Good (505a), for it is only when they know what goodness itself is that their pursuit of the *city's* good can possibly be successful. The majority are ignorant of what the Good really is, often wrongly supposing it to be pleasure (505b); hence even their best efforts to promote the good of the city are in vain.

3.9.1. The sun metaphor

Glaucon and Adeimantus urge Socrates to supply his own account of the Form of the Good, but he declines 'for the time being', on the basis that it is 'too big a topic' (506d) for the current discussion. He does, however, propose to address what he terms the 'offspring' of the Good (506e) – that is, its effects on the world – which he does by means of the extended metaphor of the sun (507b–509c). The sun, it is claimed, impacts in two highly significant ways on the physical objects – people, trees, tables, etc. – which we perceive with our senses. First, as the source of light, the sun enables these objects to be seen; as well as being visible itself, the sun is the cause of all seeing (508b), our eyes being dependent on its presence for their power to see (508c d). Second, the sun is essential to the birth, growth and nourishment of the physical realm (509b); without it, all earthly life would cease and so therefore would all manufacturing and artifice. Hence not only is the *perception* of physical things dependent on the sun, but also their *existence*.

The Form of the Good, Socrates claims, performs similar functions in the abstract realm of Forms to the sun's functions in the physical realm of Particulars. Like other Forms, the Good is an object of knowledge rather than sensory perception. Its nature is thus apprehended not through the senses but through a rational process of thought. In the same way as the sun enables its fellow physical objects to be seen, Socrates suggests, the Form of the Good enables all the other Forms to become objects of knowledge. It illuminates them for the mind's enquiries, just as the sun provides light for the eyes (508d–e). Second, and analogous to the sun's role in nourishing and sustaining other physical objects, the Good is deemed responsible for the very existence of the other Forms, which are said to owe their 'being' to the Form of the Good (509b).

Neither of these points is explained in much detail, and astonishingly it is never questioned why the object that is unconditionally good should also have such supreme significance both in epistemology (bringing about knowledge of all other Forms) and in ontology (as the cause of these Forms' existence). The sun metaphor has overtones of assigning the Form of the Good a quasi-divine status. Just as many religions assign their gods qualities of perfect or unconditional goodness, so Socrates assigns the perfectly good object in his metaphysical framework properties which are normally reserved for gods; namely, the properties of being the underlying cause of both knowledge and being. Glaucon's remark at (509c) about the Good's 'daimonic superiority' is a further indication of its godlike nature; and indeed in Book VII (517b–c) its ontological role is extended to make it the source not only of the abstract Forms, but also of light, and the sun, in the physical realm.

3.9.2. The divided line metaphor

The sun metaphor, with its account of the causal properties of the Good, is swiftly followed by another, which expounds on the difference between the intelligible and visible spheres and their respective components. This is the metaphor of the divided line (509d–511e). We are asked to picture a straight line, subject to the following divisions:

(a) The line as a whole is split into two unequal sections;
(b) Each of these is itself subdivided in two subsections, each according to the same ratio as the division of sections in (a).

The result is a line divided into two sections and four subsections, roughly as follows:

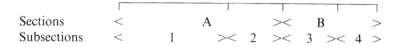

Sections   <   A   ><   B   >
Subsections   <   1   ><   2   ><   3   ><   4   >

There are two, closely related, interpretations of the meaning of the line to be found in the text. The first, introduced at (510d), treats its sections and subsections as corresponding to different types of objects. The initial division of the line into sections A and B represents the difference between the abstract objects in the intelligible realm, which are perceived with the mind rather than the senses (corresponding to section A), and the visible objects in the physical universe (section B). The further subdivision of B into 3 and 4, moreover, reflects the fact that while some visible objects (subsection 4) are mere images – shadows and reflections in water, for example – others (subsection 3) are composed of more substantial physical matter, for instance animals and plants (509e–510a).

The relative lengths of the respective parts of the line correspond, Socrates claims, to the degrees of reality or truth possessed by the associated kinds of objects (510a). Images and reflections are obviously less real than the substantial physical objects which produce them; hence 4 is shorter than 3. But equally, on the Platonic model, visible objects have less reality than intelligible ones such as Forms; therefore B is also shorter than A.

The subdivision of section A itself is trickier, and it is somewhat unclear whether Plato believes there are two distinct types of object within the intelligible realm, each with a different degree of reality. Indeed, when he addresses this subdivision (beginning 510b) he seems to change his interpretation of the line's meaning, so that each subsection now represents a category of cognitive state rather than a species of object. On this account, subsection 2 corresponds to a species of thought specifically associated with mathematics, where one reasons abstractly but on the basis of certain assumed and unquestioned hypotheses. Mathematics presupposes certain axioms as first principles, and uses them to derive conclusions about specific problems without questioning or justifying the axioms themselves (510c–d). For instance, mathematicians typically give no account of the notions of odd and even, or the different kinds of figures and angles, which are fundamental to their studies (510c). Moreover, while their investigations are abstract in the sense that they do not concern sensible physical objects but theoretical shapes and numbers, they do sometimes use visual illustrations to assist their work (510d–e). Subsection 1, on the other hand, contains the mental processes involved in philosophical dialectic. There are no unquestioned axioms here because the philosopher reasons about the nature of first principles themselves, questioning the meaning of the fundamental concepts used by all other intellectual disciplines (511b). Unlike mathematics, moreover, philosophy never makes use of visual aids – the subject operates in an entirely abstract manner, dealing with Forms rather than physical representations (511b–c).

Glaucon, in an unusually lengthy recapitulation of Socrates' position (511c–d), assigns labels to the two cognitive states relating to the intelligible realm, represented by section A of the line. The mathematician's abstract reasoning from assumed hypotheses is termed 'thought' (*dianoia*), while the philosopher's investigations of Forms issue in 'understanding' (*noēsis*). Socrates accepts these terms (511d–e) and adds two more, referring to the cognitive states concerned with objects in the visible realm (section B). The perception of substantial physical Particulars (in subsection 3) results in our forming 'belief' (*pistis*) about them, while engagement with images (subsection 4) issues in 'imagination' (*eikasia*), the contestable meaning of which I shall address presently. In total, then, four cognitive states are distinguished, each represented by a different subsection of the line.[53] These are deemed to have decreasing levels of 'clarity' as one moves from 1 to 4, corresponding to the similarly decreasing degrees of reality of the objects linked to each subsection.

There are, then, two interpretations of the line, involving categorizations of objects and related cognitive states respectively. The first interpretation, however, is somewhat problematic, since there is no clear indication of whether subsections 1 and 2 are supposed to contain two distinct kinds of objects within the intelligible realm. It would seem reasonable to place the Forms, the objects of the philosophers' knowledge, into subsection 1, where the corresponding intellectual activity is philosophical dialectic. Since subsection 2 is associated with mathematics, one might expect the corresponding objects to relate to this field of study. There is no direct textual evidence in the *Republic*, however, to suggest that Plato believes there is a set of 'mathematical' objects, distinct from the Forms, which occupy the abstract intelligible sphere. It is not certain, then, whether subsection 2 has any significance when the line is interpreted as categorizing objects rather than cognitive states.

The line's meanings may be summarized as follows:

Section	Sphere	Subsection	Object-type	Cognitive state
		1	Forms	Understanding/ knowledge
A	Intelligible			
		2	(Mathematical?)	Thought
		3	Physical Particulars	Belief
B	Visible			
		4	Images	Imagination

3.9.3. The cave metaphor

Book VII opens with perhaps the best-known passage of the *Republic*, in which Socrates introduces yet another metaphor, that of the cave and its inhabitants (514a–518b). In some respects, the cave metaphor's meaning is similar to that of the line, though there are reasons to doubt whether the two are exactly parallel. The cave passage also has a political dimension which the line lacks.

We are asked to picture a group of people bound prisoner in an underground cave, with a fire behind them and a wall in front. They are unable to turn their heads to see to their rear. Behind them, but in front of the fire, a group of puppeteers brandish a range of differently shaped objects, which they move to cast shadows on the wall in front of the prisoners. The latter, having lived their whole lives in this position, are unaware that what they are seeing is mere images, let alone of the existence of any world outside the cave (514a–515c). Socrates describes a possible ascent, however, in which certain prisoners break free from their shackles and, once they become accustomed to the fire's glare, become cognizant of the other objects in the cave: the puppets, puppet-masters and indeed the fire itself (515c–e). In their next step, some of them are able to venture outside the cave into the sunlight; though their eyes find this environment difficult at first, and they must get used to looking at images of things in shadows and reflections before being able directly to view the original objects themselves (516a). In the final stage of their progression, however, they not only perceive the *bona fide* objects of nature first hand, but can look directly into the source of light, namely the sun (516b).

Socrates does not explicitly give meanings for all elements of this story. He does state at the outset that it is a metaphor for the effects of education (513e), and later says that it should be 'fitted together with what went before' (517b), seemingly referring to the divided line. He thereupon states that the cave equates to the visible world (section B of the line) and the journey outside of it represents the progression to the intelligible (section A). The fire inside the cave, moreover, is equivalent to the actual sun, the source of light for our visible realm, and the metaphoric sun in the world outside the cave symbolizes the Form of the Good (ibid.).

Now, given the alleged correspondence between the cave and line metaphors, and the latter's division into subsections 1 to 4, many interpretations of the *Republic* treat certain features of the cave narrative as denoting the same psychological states as are demarcated by the line's four subsections. For example, within the visible realm denoted by the cave, the cognitive state of imagination (*eikasia*), induced by perceiving mere images of physical objects, corresponds to the situation of the prisoners looking at shadows on the cave wall. By contrast, belief (*pistis*), issuing from the perception of actual physical Particulars, is illustrated by the condition of former prisoners who have broken their bonds and can see the actual artefacts inside the cave; including the fire, which we know represents the physical sun. In terms of the line's divisions, then, the bound prisoners seem to correspond to the cognitive states in subsection 4, while those who can view the full interior of the cave are connoted with subsection 3. Similarly, in the intelligible realm pictured metaphorically as the world outside the cave, the cognitive state of thought (*dianoia*) accessed by mathematicians may be symbolized by the people who, unaccustomed to sunlight, view shadows and reflections in water rather than solid natural objects. These, then, correspond to subsection 2 of the line. Finally, philosophers who gain understanding (*noēsis*) of the Forms (the cognitive state in subsection 1) are denoted by those who view the real objects in the outside world, the most experienced of whom can also see the metaphoric sun, i.e. can understand the Form of the Good, directly.

A neat interpretation of the cave metaphor is available, then, as charting the progress of someone who begins by looking at images of physical things (the bound prisoner/subsection 4), before progressing to observe physical things themselves (the untied cave dweller/ subsection 3). Later, he advances to engage with the intelligible realm (outside the cave), where he first engages in mathematical reasoning from assumed first principles (looks at reflections/subsection 2), before further progressing to study the fundamental Forms (sees real objects/subsection 1), culminating in the Form of the Good (the sun). Such a view makes good sense of Socrates' remark that the cave analogy fits with what went previously (the line).

There is a major difficulty with this account, however, which stems primarily from Socrates' comment (515a) that the prisoners in the cave are 'like us'. Applied to the above analysis, this would suggest that the majority of people spend their lives engaged in viewing and responding to images; to use Plato's examples, shadows, reflections in water and smooth shiny materials, and 'everything of that sort' (509e–510a). Such a suggestion, however, seems quite absurd. Even overlooking the question of how many people make genuine contact with the abstract intelligible realm, which is admittedly limited to mathematicians and philosophers, it is surely the case that practically all of us constantly perceive and engage with actual physical objects, rather than simply the images of these things.

This point relates to a more general problem with using the term 'imagination' (*eikasia*) to label subsection 4 of the divided line. Insofar as this term refers to the psychological states associated with visual perceptions of images, it is hard to understand what important category of mental phenomenon, worthy of its own label, this is meant to delineate. It is difficult, that is, to identify any specific type of experience or thought that is always and only associated with seeing shadows or reflections; as Annas puts it; such image-perception 'seems not to correspond to anything significant in our lives'.[54]

In order to make sense, then, of the claim that most of us are like the cave's prisoners, whilst maintaining their association with the state of 'imagination' (*eikasia*), we must interpret this term more broadly than Plato's examples in Book VI suggest. In other words, we should take *eikasia* to mean more than just a response to the visual perception of images. Cross and Woozley[55] suggest that it can refer to any mental state in which 'likeness is accepted as reality, without any realisation that it is a likeness'. Now, the claim on Socrates' part that most people frequently subscribe to thoughts of this kind would fit with other elements of the *Republic*. For example, when Plato discusses the impact of the arts on society in Book X, he describes a common tendency to regard artworks as reliable guides to truth. This might involve, for example, treating a picture of an object as giving an accurate reflection of its properties, or, more seriously, taking the pronouncements of the poets on topics such as history, theology, human nature or virtue as authoritative on these matters. In fact, Socrates argues, artists do nothing more than provide their own, often mistaken, impressions or likenesses of physical objects, or (in the case of poets) human qualities and behaviour. However, those whose education is based primarily on the arts, such as the Athenians with their strict diet of Homer and other tragic poetry, often become incapable of distinguishing the misleading claims made in such works from reality.[56] They are effectively confined to engaging with the 'images' of the world which these artworks contain, and, like the tied prisoners, remain unaware of the fact that they *are* only images, let alone that there are other more reliable sources of truth elsewhere.

One way, then, to treat Socrates' analogy between the majority of people and the prisoners in the cave is as a complaint about over-reliance on the arts in education. Another possible reading – somewhat speculative as there is no direct textual evidence – is to take *eikasia* to refer to a common tendency to form judgements on the basis of how the visible world and its objects immediately *appear*, rather than any more sophisticated scientific investigations. The prisoner metaphor might then stand for the uneducated person's reliance on his intuitive responses to the surface appearances of objects, which he wrongly treats as being informative about physical reality. For example, someone might instinctively think that the earth is flat on the basis that it seems this way to his senses, though the most rudimentary study of astronomy would soon show him otherwise. Similarly, many (including Aristotle) have held that matter is continuous and infinitely divisible into smaller and smaller pieces – a view which coheres with appearance and intuition, but which has been proven false by developments in atomic theory.

The progression from being compelled to look at shadows on the cave wall to being free within the cave and observing all its contents might thus be taken to correspond to the shift from the uneducated person's reliance on intuitive perception of the sensible realm, to a more reliable grasp of physical nature based on education in the natural sciences: physics, chemistry, biology and so on. However, there is a further move to be made, on Plato's model, from engagement with the physical even at this more sophisticated level, to the recognition of the abstract – which is attained through studying mathematics and philosophy. This is represented metaphorically by the journey from the cave itself to the world outside.

3.9.4. The guardians' curriculum

The material in Book VII[57] dealing with the ways in which philosophy should and should not be practised has been addressed in section 3.8.4. What remains is a detailed exposition of the stages of training a potential guardian must undergo. This begins (521d–522b) with a background in music, poetry and physical education, subject to the conditions outlined in Books II–III. Next, Socrates proposes, should come education in various branches of mathematics: arithmetic (522c–526c), plane and solid geometry (526c–528d), astronomy (528d–530d) and harmonics (530d–531c). Their purpose is to provide preparatory grounding for the next stage of the guardians' training, which is in philosophical dialectic.

Mathematics is akin to philosophy in that it involves abstract reasoning, albeit, as Book VI explains, reasoning based on assumed hypotheses rather than in pursuit of first principles. By studying mathematics in its purest, most abstract versions, Plato believes the mind is raised from its focus on the sensible material realm to engage for the first time with the intelligible world of concepts. In terms of the line metaphor, mathematical thought occupies subsection 2; in the cave analogy – specifically recalled at (532b–c) – it is the state of looking at reflections of objects in the world outside the cave, which is a necessary precursor to looking directly at the objects themselves.

Mathematics, then, sharpens the conceptual mind, preparing it for philosophical study (526b–c). Moreover, while maths has numerous practical applications, not least in war (526d), Socrates argues that the focus of its study should not primarily be on these, but rather on solving purely conceptual problems, for it is the latter which provide the necessary bridge between studying the sensible world and engaging with the Forms. So, for example, when astronomy and harmonics are taught, the emphasis must not be on the movements of the physical planets (530b–c), or on musical notes (531a–b). Rather, these sensible phenomena should be taken as mere models for an abstract study of motion, which dispenses with empirical observation and proceeds on the basis of theoretical reasoning alone.

Only after a background in mathematics are the trainee guardians able to access subsection 1 of the line or – in cave terms – to make direct observations of objects in the sunlight. They finally do so, undergoing their instruction in philosophical dialectic; the purpose of which is to acquaint them which the nature of the Forms, including ultimately the Form of the Good (532a–b). This vital part of their preparation for government should, we are later told, last for about five years (539e), following which they must serve a successful 15 years in a subsidiary political role, before they are ready to become *bona fide* rulers, aged approximately 50 (540a).

3.9.5. The philosopher in politics: 'Return to the Cave'

The cave metaphor remains a highly contentious element of the *Republic*, open to numerous interpretations. Besides its relevance to Plato's philosophy of education it also bears on his political thought, in particular the theory of the philosopher-ruler. Socrates more than once uses the metaphor to illustrate the trained philosophers' transition from immersion in abstract theoretical study to practical involvement in the life of the *polis*. This is described in terms of their returning from the sunlit world outside the cave, back into the cave itself, where they are obliged to engage once more with the prisoners (i.e. the mass of uneducated citizens) in their functions as officials, and later as outright governors.[58]

Someone who has journeyed outside the cave and witnessed the external world is, Socrates admits, likely to 'behave awkwardly' and even appear 'completely ridiculous' (517d) when returning to converse with those who have spent their entire lives imprisoned and looking at shadows. This corresponds to the point that philosophers trained in theoretical reasoning may find it hard to operate in the sphere of practical politics, struggling to explain their points to people who have no understanding of philosophical concepts. Plato's response to this is to say that the only reason philosophers *appear* practically inept is that they have, in metaphorical terms, come from light into darkness. They deal awkwardly with political matters only because they are operating at a higher intellectual level which those unacquainted with Forms are unable to comprehend.

Once philosophers are assigned supreme authority within a state, however, they can remodel political and social organizations according to their own design, and hence no longer be forced to operate with flawed rules and practices such as those of Athens, which are tailored to the ignorant rather than the wise. Far from being ineffective in government, moreover, the philosophers' understanding of the Forms, particularly that of the Good, provides an ideal basis for political action (540a).

Even if philosophers are *capable* of governing well there is another important point, also raised by the cave metaphor, which concerns their *willingness* to do so. Those who have been outside the cave will naturally feel reluctant to return there: 'their souls are always pressing upwards, eager to spend their time above' (517c). Correspondingly, a philosopher who has experienced the pleasures of the contemplative life is likely to find his return to practical affairs burdensome; indeed, it is in his philosophical nature to 'despise' political rule (521b).

One might wonder, though this seemingly did not occur to Plato, whether the philosopher's intrinsic dislike of government might diminish the likelihood of his ruling efficiently. Plato's own position is that on the contrary, reluctant politicians are far less dangerous than those who actively desire to rule, since the latter will squabble for power to the overall detriment of the state (521a–b). The philosopher's reluctance to govern does, however, raise the question of what motivates him to perform his allotted task. Socrates apparently suggests (519d) that a philosopher would not rule voluntarily but must be compelled to do so, contrary to his wishes. He is obliged to use his knowledge of the Good, provided by his city, to further the city's welfare, and he may be justly forced into doing so even though his own preference is for philosophical contemplation.

The question of the philosophers' apparent lack of motivation for political activity brings into focus two more general issues in Plato's ethical theory, raised previously in section 3.6.3. The first concerned the relationship between being just in the Socratic sense of one's soul being governed by its rational part, and in the conventional sense of behaving fairly and dutifully towards others. The philosopher, we can assume, is a paradigm case of Socratic justice, as his rigorous intellectual training has developed his intellectual faculties and imbued in him a love of truth and knowledge, the goals specifically associated with reason. Indeed, Socrates explicitly says that the philosopher is 'a friend and relative of truth, justice, courage and moderation' (487a). There is a question, however, about whether his peculiar psychological makeup necessarily results in his being conventionally just. It might seem, on the contrary, that his strong preference for private contemplation might make him indisposed to benefit others or fulfil his duties to society. The second problem raised by the philosopher's reluctance to return to the cave involves the link between having an individually just soul, in the Socratic sense, and playing one's role within the politically just city. The latter, we know, requires fulfilling the task most suited to one's aptitude and training. But again, if the individually just life is that of an otherworldly philosopher buried in abstract study, there is a clear tension between this and the performance of the political role of a guardian.

Socrates offers a partial solution to these problems (520a–e), where he appears to adjust the earlier suggestion that philosophers should be coerced into government. Instead, he suggests they might be persuaded by force of argument that it is just and right for them to fulfil their political duties. One argument which might be put to them centres on the debt of gratitude they owe to the state, which has educated them at great expense, providing them with knowledge inaccessible to the vast majority. In return for this, it is argued, they should offer something back to the state, utilizing their special knowledge and abilities to its overall benefit (520b–c). The philosophers should also recognize that if they refuse the job of government, it will be taken over by another more power-hungry group who will harm the interests of the city (520c–d). These arguments should, Socrates claims, be sufficient to induce the philosophers into government; they will not refuse, Glaucon agrees, because they are 'just people' who are asked to carry out 'just orders' (520e).

This passage implies possible connections between the philosophers' individual Socratic justice, on the one hand, and both their conventional justice and their participation in the just state on the other. These connections are as follows. First, since a philosopher is a rational person who has been trained to appreciate and respond to moral arguments, he will be susceptible to persuasion by rational means into doing his duty, i.e. what is conventionally just. Someone who was less thoughtful and driven by their spirit or appetite might fail to appreciate their debt of gratitude, but the philosophically trained mind perceives clearly what is required of it. Secondly, the philosopher's dominant reasoning faculty, which 'calculates about better and worse' (see 441b–c), informs him that it is 'better' that he, rather than a lover of power, should govern the state; thus 'doing his own' as political justice dictates.

The issue of the philosopher's political involvement poses a further problem, however, for the overall thesis of the *Republic*. Plato's main project is to show how and why being just is in an agent's self-interest. Now, in the philosopher's case, it seems that justice requires him to take a position in government. A critic might argue that the philosopher's own interests are *not* promoted by acting in this way. Rather, the best life for the philosopher is to remain in the world outside the metaphorical cave, exercising his intellect in the contemplation of Forms and the discovery of fundamental truths, and avoiding altogether the tiresome business of politicking and administrative bureaucracy. There is, then, an apparent contradiction within Plato's theory. On the one hand, he wants to claim that being just is always in one's interests; but on the other it seems that by doing what is just, i.e. governing the state, a philosopher sacrifices his own interests for the good of others.[59]

Nicholas White[60] argues that this case is, indeed, an exception to Plato's general rule that being just promotes one's personal advantage: the philosopher's return to the cave is just, White believes, but disadvantageous from his own perspective. If this were really so, however, and Plato acknowledged the point, we would perhaps expect more reference to this in the text. Surely Glaucon or Adeimantus, for example, would be moved to point out that, in this one instance at least, Socrates has been unable to show that the just life and the happy one coincide.

Other commentators have sought ways to defend the proposition that by returning to the cave and fulfilling the requirements of justice, the philosopher-ruler does, after all, further his own well-being. I shall briefly address two of them.

C. D. C. Reeve[61] proposes that the problem might be solved by distinguishing between the philosopher's interests in the short term and the long term. A philosophical soul might prefer to contemplate abstract concepts than to engage in practical politics; however, Socrates also says (520d, 521b) that the consequence of philosophers' refusal to govern would be a disordered state with civil war between rival factions. Reeve plausibly argues that in such a city there would be little opportunity to practise philosophy, as the social scene would be dominated by internecine conflict. Indeed, one could say more generally that it is only by engaging in politics and ensuring a well-governed state that philosophers can guarantee the resources and the political will to continue providing facilities for philosophical education and research. Hence, it is argued, the rational course for a philosopher who wants to maximize his life-long opportunity for private study is to participate in government and ensure that the city's educational establishments remain oper-ative and well-funded. Thus, by doing what is just (i.e. governing the city) he also promotes, in the long term, his self-interest. It is notable that when describing the philosopher-ruler's life at the end of Book VII (540b), Socrates seems to suggest he will combine study of the Forms with his political duties. This coheres with Reeve's idea that by contributing a certain amount of time to government, he enables himself to spend other periods doing what he enjoys most, namely philosophizing.

There are difficulties, however, with using this argument to show that ruling the city is in philosophers' best interests. First, the idea that they can use their role to promote academic institutions for their own enjoyment is never mentioned by Plato as a reason for accept-ing their task; his emphasis is rather on their governing because they regard it as the just thing to do (520d–e). Second, there is a 'free rider' problem. Granted that if *all* philosophers refused to govern, the civic order would break down and no one would any longer prac-tise philosophy; there is still a question as to whether it is rational for each individual philosopher, calculating his own interests, to volun-teer his services in government. It could be argued, for instance, that an individual philosopher's best option is to free-ride off the contri-butions his fellow philosophers make to the city, whilst spending as much of his own time as possible in private study. Admittedly, it may be wise for him to give the *appearance* of working for the good of the state, so as to escape public censure, but having done this, surely he is best off covertly focusing his attention on philosophy instead of public affairs?

A second explanation of how justice and self-interest might coin-cide in the philosopher's case is proposed by Richard Kraut.[62] This appeals primarily to a passage in Book VI (500b–501b), where Socrates claims that a philosopher who studies the Forms is attracted by their orderliness; the fact that they are 'organized and always the same' and 'neither do injustice nor suffer it, being all in a rational order'. The philosopher's love of the Forms, moreover, motivates him to 'imitate' them and 'try to become as like them as he can' (500c). In other words, his study of the most rational and ordered objects in existence implants in him the desire to become as much like them as possible; that is, to lead a rational and well-ordered life. This orderliness includes, on Kraut's understanding,[63] the idea of reciprocity: a philosopher will seek balanced relationships with others in which one favour is returned with another, where all debts are repaid, and where there is mutual honesty and fulfilled expectations. Such interactions please him, Kraut claims, because their harmonious nature reminds him of his most beloved objects, the Forms. Also, as a lover of order, a philosopher will wish to promote balance and harmony within his city.

Kraut argues that by playing a role in government, a philosopher fulfils his deep-seated desires for order, which amounts to imitation of the Forms. He achieves order in his relationships with others by repaying his debt of gratitude to his state. He also implants order in the state itself by ensuring that it is appropriately administered and that everyone else fulfils their allotted tasks. Thus, in returning to the cave, the philosopher does indeed further his own well-being, conceived in terms of living an orderly life, akin to the Forms, against the backdrop of a state which his governance renders similarly well-ordered. And since, as we have seen, governing the state is also the *just* course of action for him, the link between acting justly and promoting one's self-interest can be successfully maintained.

Kraut's argument is ingenious, and explains how both being conventionally just and contributing to a just state might coincide with a philosopher's self-interest. It does, however, involve reading in a highly detailed account of what it means to 'imitate the Forms' in one's own life. A critic might argue that the pursuit of orderliness in one's soul need not involve seeking ethical relations with the rest of one's society, so much as following a rational plan or programme; and this might well be one of private study rather than participation in a political realm where reason and order are frequently absent. Moreover, although Socrates explicitly states (500c) that a philosopher desires to render *himself* as similar as possible to the Forms, he never actually says that he necessarily wants his *state* to be similarly constituted. All he does say, at (500d), is that should a philosopher be compelled to govern, his knowledge of the Forms will render him a good 'craftsman' of a virtuous society. There is no direct indication that this is something he himself wants to do to further his self-interest.

Discussion questions:
(a) What sense can be made of the suggestion that many people spend their lives engaging with images?
(b) Is mathematics a good preparation for studying philosophy?
(c) To what extent should we demand that political leaders sacrifice their own happiness for the good of the state?

3.10. THE CATEGORIES OF INJUSTICE (543a–576b)

At the beginning of *Republic* VIII, Plato returns to tackle a project he had alluded to at the end of Book IV. This was to analyse the various possible types of *unjust* state and soul, and their differences from the just ones outlined in *Republic* IV. In Books VIII and IX, he describes four unjust states and four correspondingly unjust souls, manifesting various degrees of divergence from the ideal. Throughout his accounts of these, he maintains the close analogies established in Book IV between the component parts of a city and those of a human psyche. To recap, the just state involved the guardian class – who have since been identified as trained philosophers – governing with the assistance of auxiliaries (soldiers) over the productive workers. Correspondingly, the just soul was one in which reason had overall charge, and allied itself with spirit in order to exercise rule over the various appetites. This section begins by laying out, in schematic form, Plato's accounts of the four unjust states and souls, and noting how the analogy between their respective components plays out in this taxonomy.

3.10.1. Taxonomies of states and souls

The four unjust types of city, in increasing order of injustice, are categorized as follows:
    a. **Timocracy** (545c–548d): a city ruled by its warrior class, rather than by philosopher-guardians, which consequently pursues warlike policies and engages in some oppression of its own people.
    b. **Oligarchy** (500d–553a): government in the hands of a wealthy subset of the productive class, namely money-makers and businessmen, who govern in their own financial self-interest.
    c. **Democracy** (555b–558c): a state in which any member can participate equally, according to his wishes, in a governmental role, and which is 'full of freedom and freedom of speech' (557b).

d. **Tyranny** (562a–569c): a state with a single ruthless dictator, who maintains his position by force and fear.

The corresponding soul-types, also increasingly unjust, are thus characterised:

a. **Timocratic** (548d–550c): spirit (*thumos*) has precedence over both reason and appetite, producing 'a proud and honour-loving man' (550b).

b. **Oligarchic** (553a–555a): the soul is governed by its appetite for wealth, but the other appetites are at least reined in to some degree, leading to a careful and orderly albeit highly materialistic character.

c. **Democratic** (561c–d): the full array of appetites is allowed to influence behaviour, leading to a disordered life in which a variety of different activities are pursued, but without any tenacity or overall purpose.

d. **Tyrannical** (571a–580c): the soul is dominated by the very worst kind of 'lawless' appetite, a species of lust (*erōs*). Total ruthlessness is shown in pursuing its satisfactions, which are mostly sexual, often perverse and sometimes violent.

For purposes of the state-soul analogy, we can again see that, as guardian-rulers correspond to reason, so auxiliaries match up to spirit, and producers to appetites. Of this last group, moreover, the most wealthy producers are now likened specifically to appetites for money, and the most wicked – those who become tyrant rulers – are deemed analogous to lust.

It need not be assumed that in Plato's view every state or soul that is unjust falls neatly into one of these four categories. Indeed, he explicitly says with regard to cities that some existing ones are 'intermediate' between the categories outlined, for example dynasties and purchased kingships (544c–d). We can probably assume something similar applies to souls; that is, many do not fit exactly into any of the four paradigms, but contain elements of more than one, or are somewhere in between. The fourfold categorization does, though, provide us with a theoretical scheme to highlight the most important kinds of difference between constitutions and between human psychologies respectively. It also offers a scheme by which to evaluate existing states and souls; assuming we agree with Plato's ordering, we can judge all constitutions, and human beings, by considering which of the paradigm types they most resemble.

Socrates presents the four types of corrupt state and soul by describing their occurrence through processes of degeneration, where in both cases justice becomes timocracy, timocracy slides into oligarchy, oligarchy is reduced to democracy and finally democracy descends into tyranny. In the political version of the narrative, a single city is viewed as declining over the course of time through the various stages of corruption, from a just state to a tyrannical one. In the story of the soul, the different stages are pictured as occurring in successive generations of a dynasty: a just person is father to a timocrat, who in turn fathers an oligarch, until we arrive at the tyrannical son of a democratic father. It need not be assumed, however, that Plato believes there is anything inevitable about the processes of degeneration he describes. If there were, after all, then every city would eventually become a tyranny, and every family would end up producing tyrannical offspring, neither of which is remotely plausible. We should, then, treat both degenerative stories chiefly as vehicles for presenting the different kinds of city and soul.

In what follows, I shall examine the low ranking that is assigned to democracy, both as a species of political constitution and as a human character-type. It is significant that, in both cases, Plato rates democracy below oligarchy. In the political context, this means that a state where every citizen is permitted to participate in government is regarded as worse, all things considered, than one controlled by a wealthy elite seeking to maximize its own profits. To many modern western readers, this might seem a bizarre ordering, so it is important to consider the model of democracy that Plato so strongly condemns, and his reasons for doing so.

3.10.2. The critique of political democracy

The two most significant features of political democracy, as characterized in Book VIII, are freedom and equality. Freedom was an essential tenet of the Greek conception of democracy; Aristotle, in his *Politics*, states that democratic systems are characterized primarily by 'the sovereignty of the majority, and liberty' (1310a30). Of particular importance was freedom of speech (*isēgoria*); in Athens, everyone (or more precisely, every male citizen) had the right to speak at the Assembly and thereby have some input into the decision-making process. The other principal characteristic of democracy, as emphasized in *Republic* VIII, is the conviction that every person is of equal value; as Plato puts it, the distribution of 'equality to both equals and unequals alike' (558c).

Plato's objections to democracy are manifold, and are expressed in Book VIII (555b–558c) and (562b–563e) in the form of bitingly satirical descriptions of life in a democratic city. Foremost among his complaints is this city's lack of unity. In oligarchy, where the wealthy rule in their own class-interest, disunity stems from the formation of two warring factions, the rich and poor (551d). But in democracy, disunity is even greater, as each individual citizen does exactly as they like without any concern for pursuing any common goals: 'there is no requirement to rule, even if you're capable of it, or again to be ruled if you don't want to be, or to be at war when the others are, or at peace unless you happen to want it' (557e). The freedom of action typical of such states prevents any communality of purpose among their citizens. Even worse, it may lead to a situation where obedience to the law itself becomes unfashionable; the culture of 'do what you will' may become so strong that it is considered slavish to submit to any legal authority, leading to a breakdown in law and order (563d–e).

Another strand in Plato's attack on democracy involves the inappropriate equality of privileges that are granted, both to participate in the political process and more generally to enjoy the freedom of the city. These are assigned, in Plato's view, without regard for suitability, desert or adverse consequences. Thus, we are told, condemned criminals 'stay on at the centre of things' (558a), 'a foreign visitor is made equal to a citizen' (562e–563a), and 'slaves [. . .] are no less free than those who bought them' (563b). Even animals are permitted 'to roam freely and proudly along the street' (563c), though this point may be included largely for satirical impact. Plato certainly believes that education is an important sphere in which the democratic obsession with freedom and equality has a negative impact. As there are few, if any, accepted educational hierarchies, parents and teachers can exercise very little control over how their children or pupils behave, and respect for those in senior positions is scant. Plato waxes lyrical on this theme: 'a father accustoms himself to behave like a child and fear his sons' (562e); 'a teacher is afraid of his students and flatters them, while the students despise their teachers and tutors' (563a). This perhaps familiar critique of liberal education methods is particularly significant when we recall the central role that education played within the just state. The guardians must be trained by their elders and betters, and show respect for their knowledge and experience, if they are to become proficient rulers.

The conception of democracy that Plato chooses to attack in Book VIII is a very extreme one, more akin to what we might call anarchy than democracy as recognized today. We might also question the extent to which Plato's vitriol is accurately targeted on the Athenian democratic system under which he lived. The historical Athens was very dissimilar to the caricatured 'democratic' state described in Book VIII.[64] Rather than being all-inclusive in terms of political involvement, Athens excluded women, slaves, foreigners and those with foreign parents from membership of its decision-making bodies. Far from being the epitome of tolerance, Athens sometimes drove out those who expressed controversial views: the philosopher Protagoras suffered this fate, and Socrates was put to death partly for his 'impious' opinions. Again, instead of witnessing a breakdown in respect for the law, Athens exacted stern retribution upon perceived offenders, as Socrates himself discovered to his cost.

It seems, then, that a defender of democracy might reasonably accuse Plato of attacking a straw man, since a democratic society need not have anything like the extreme liberal and egalitarian features he lampoons. Indeed, very few states as free and inclusive as the one he condemns have ever existed in practice, and his own Athenian democracy was certainly not among them. Whilst, then, his points serve adequately to warn against the dangers of taking individual freedom and political equality to extremes, insofar as they are levelled at democracy *per se* they involve a somewhat misleading caricature of what such a system must entail. Of course, advocates of democracy may also disagree with Plato's negative evaluation of those features of the system he *does* accurately depict. In particular, they might dispute his assumption that a unified society where everyone works to benefit the state is preferable to a pluralistic system in which people are free to pursue their own conceptions of what is valuable. Equally, his critics might assert a greater intrinsic equality of merit between citizens of different social classes, which justifies giving them greater power than Plato saw fit.

3.10.3. Psychological democracy versus oligarchy

I shall now turn to the rank-ordering of souls. The just one, as outlined in Book IV, is governed by its rational part: the faculty best fitted to make decisions about the person's best interests. A soul that is dominated by spirit – the timocratic type – is unjust, as it tends to be warlike, obstinate, harsh to inferiors, and overly concerned with victory, honour and rank (548e–549b). A soul in which appetite predominates is worse still, and there are three types of appetitive soul in Plato's taxonomy. Of these, I will focus here on the two least maladjusted (and probably most common): the oligarch and the democrat. I shall address the worst, the tyrannical type, in section 3.11.1.

The distinction between the oligarchic and democratic characters hinges on a contrast between the different types of appetite foremost in each. The oligarch is ruled by what Plato calls *necessary* appetites. These are defined as desires (a) which are intrinsic to all human beings, and (b) whose satisfaction is, on the whole, beneficial to the individual concerned (558d–e). In particular, it appears, an oligarchic man is typified by his love of material and financial security. He is 'a thrifty worker', a 'profiteer' and a 'hoarder' (554a), whose life is dedicated to the acquisition of material goods but who is not given to extravagance or hedonism. The democrat, by contrast, gives free rein to what are termed *unnecessary* appetites, which are neither essential to humanity nor contribute to his interests; examples include gastronomic, spendthrift and certain sexual desires (559b–c). However, the democrat is not exclusively dedicated to sensual or materialistic pleasure. In particular, when he grows older he is likely to afford equal status to *all* his desires, necessary and unnecessary (561a–d). This results in a lifestyle where he pursues a variety of different goals, either simultaneously, or for successive short periods of time after which one interest is replaced by another. These interests could include anything from feasting to dieting, exercise to relaxation, money-making, politics, war or even 'what he takes to be philosophy' (561d).

Dominic Scott (2000) raises the question of why the democrat, thus characterized, is regarded as being further from justice than the oligarch. After all, while the latter seeks only material wealth, the former has a wider range of ends, some of which – like political involvement and philosophical discussion – we might expect Plato to approve of. One reason for the democrat's lower ranking, however, involves the issue of psychological unity.[65] Justice was characterized, in Book IV, in terms of harmony within the soul and an absence of civil war between its various elements. Now it appears that the democrat, who is a 'complex man, full of all sorts of characters [. . .] and ways of living' (561e), has less unity of purpose and is likely to experience greater conflicts of motivation than the oligarch who is dedicated solely to material security and keeps his other appetites in check (554c). Plato argues, moreover, that the oligarch's overriding concern for money imposes at least an outward 'respectability' (554e) on his behaviour. He avoids voluptuousness and hedonistic excess because it is too costly, and is careful to avoid acquiring a bad reputation which would jeopardize his finances. He generally refrains then from dishonest or aggressive actions, not because he is concerned with doing good *per se*, but because he fears the personal consequences of being caught out in wrongdoing. He acts wrongfully only when he can do so 'with impunity' and where it benefits him monetarily (554c). By contrast, since the democrat is interested in a wider range of pleasures and is less afraid of compromising his financial well-being, there is perhaps a greater likelihood of rapaciousness or vice in his dealings with others.

One might still wonder, however, whether the democratic individual's pursuit of political, military and even philosophic goals means that he is not exclusively governed by his appetitive part. Rather, one might suggest, the wide range of motivations to which he subscribes also includes some spirited ones, which lead him occasionally to participate in the public arena, and some rational ones, resulting in sporadic engagement with philosophical study. If this is so, it is debatable whether Plato is right to view him as inferior, in terms of justice, to the wholly appetite-driven oligarch.

Scott's answer to this[66] is that the democrat's intermittent dalliances with philosophy and politics are not actually the work of his reason and spirit, but rather of quasi-appetites, amounting to whims or fancies, whereby he happens to find these activities temporarily pleasant or diverting. Note, for example, the way the democrat's philosophical activity is described (561d); he 'occupies himself with what he takes to be philosophy'. Now, this need not imply the love of learning which typifies the rational part of the soul (see 581b). Rather, it may simply be an enjoyment of intellectual exercise, word play, or the cut and thrust of debate: forms of *amusement* that result from doing philosophy, rather than the knowledge thereby attained. A similar account might be given of a democrat's involvement in political life. 'He often engages in politics', we are told, 'leaping up from his seat and saying and doing whatever comes into his mind' (562d). A timocratic character, who is motivated by spirit, would practise politics to further his reputation and gain honour, but the democrat again seems merely to dabble for the sake of amusement or distraction. Equally, he takes an interest in warfare 'if he happens to admire soldiers' (ibid.): a childish wish-fulfilment derived from hero-worship, rather than any serious motivation to pursue victory in combat.

In summary, Scott's thesis is that although the democratic individual occasionally pursues the same activities as those whose souls are dominated by higher faculties, his motivations to engage in them do not stem from reason or spirit, as they do not ultimately issue from desires for knowledge or honour. Rather, the democrat is a pleasure seeker who just so happens, on occasion, to enjoy philosophy, politics, or war.

3.10.4. Residents of the unjust cities

Questions might be raised about the relation between, on the one hand, the sorts of people who live in and govern the various types of degenerate state and, on the other, the corresponding degenerate souls. Towards the beginning of Book VIII, Socrates suggests that political constitutions are born from 'the characters of the people who live in the cities governed by them' (544d). Taken literally, this could imply that a just city will be populated by just people, a timocratic city by timocrats and so on, with the nature of the state in each case issuing from that of its people. There is, however, plenty of evidence both in the text and from common sense for doubting that this can be so.

In section 3.6.3., doubts were expressed over whether the just city is comprised entirely of just individuals. In particular, it seemed unlikely that members of the productive class could be individually just in Plato's sense, as they are not deemed sufficiently rational to govern their own affairs. There are similar or even greater problems, moreover, in claiming that the various degenerate city-types are made up of people with equivalent psychologies. Taking Plato's description of the timocratic state, on the one hand we see that it manifests a 'love of victory and love of honour' (548c), which suggests the presence of some timocratic, spirit-dominated souls within it. However, we are also told that the leaders of a timocracy 'enslave and hold as serfs and servants those whom they previously guarded as free friends and providers of upkeep' (547b), implying that while the leaders themselves might have the proud, dominant attributes of the timocratic character, the timocratic *state* also incorporates a productive class, containing different character-types who are subjugated to do the rulers' bidding. In political oligarchy, likewise, it seems that the leaders, though not necessarily the rank and file, match the description of the oligarchic soul. The people who run this state are rich, businesslike characters who epitomize the oligarchic love of wealth, coupled with some prudential self-restraint. But, again, the oligarchic state also contains some who 'squander their property' (552b), and thereafter contribute nothing to the society but become beggars or criminals. As spendthrifts, these characters do not fit the oligarchic model – in fact they appear more like democrats.

The democratic constitution itself is described as being 'embroidered with every kind of character-type' (557c); the freedom each person possesses means that 'one finds people of all varieties' (557b) in this state. This suggests that whilst there will be some whose souls are themselves democratic – that is, overrun by a mix of necessary and unnecessary appetites – there could equally be others with different psychologies; some oligarchs, some tyrants, perhaps even some timocrats and just individuals. The last, no doubt, will rail against the state's organization, as Socrates did against the Athenian democracy, but they could still exist within it, albeit denied what Plato considers their proper function as rulers. Once again, therefore, the democratic state is not populated exclusively by democratic people. When we come to the tyrannical state, moreover, it seems patently absurd to say that everyone living under such a regime is himself a psychological tyrant, driven by uncontrollable lust. Indeed, it is hardly possible to imagine a society of tyrannical souls existing without degenerating into anarchy.

To summarize it is implausible to claim that each type of city consists entirely of people with the corresponding psychological character. There are indeed problems in claiming this for any of the cities Plato outlines. In seeking to understand his remark that constitutions issue from the characters of the people within them, however, we might consider a different thesis, namely that the *rulers* of each type of state have the associated type of soul. Certainly the philosophers, who govern the just state, seem also to be Socratically just in that their souls are dominated by reason and orientated towards knowledge. Equally, the timocratic state appears to be led by timocratic characters: spirited warriors who direct policy towards honour and warfare. The oligarchic state, once more, is ruled by psychological oligarchs: money-minded businessmen who govern for profit. Unfortunately, this correspondence breaks down when we arrive at democracy. In a democratic state, everyone, regardless of their character, can play a part in ruling; and any official posts are determined by lot (561b). The city's inhabitants are a hotchpotch of different characters, not all of whom need fit the model of the democratic soul. It follows, then, that many who govern in a democracy are not themselves psychological democrats. Rather, the 'rulers' of such a city, insofar as any exist, are many and varied.

Finally, as regards tyranny, Plato does assert (575c) that a tyrant ruler 'has in his soul the greatest and strongest tyrant of all'. This is rather problematic, though, when we consider what having a tyrannical soul actually entails. Such a character is dominated by 'lawless appetite' (571b), a lust for extreme, mostly sexual and often sadistic forms of pleasure. But as Annas argues,[67] it is far from clear that all political tyrants have this kind of personality. There are some who have – for instance Caligula – but generally such people are unlikely to be successful dictators, as they are too depraved and chaotic to formulate workable strategies for retaining power. Indeed, if any of Plato's types of soul seems most likely to be dictator material, it is probably the spirit-centred timocratic, whose dominant faculty is 'wholly dedicated to the pursuit of control, victory and high repute' (581a).

Whilst, then, it is both plausible and consistent with Plato's text to say that the characters of the three 'best' political constitutions reflect those of the people who govern them, there are problems in applying this either to democracy or tyranny. Hence, although Plato's accounts of political and psychological injustice successfully sustain his analogies between states and souls, and between their component parts, it is more difficult to assimilate his comment (544d) that the nature of each state derives from those of the individuals living there.

Discussion question:
In what ways might some societies take the ideals of (a) freedom and (b) equality too far?

3.11. THE DEFENCE OF JUSTICE REVISITED (576b–592b)

This section begins by focusing on Plato's sketch of the tyrannical character, considering how he uses it to help address his central question in the *Republic* – why it is in our interests to be just rather than unjust.

3.11.1. The tyrant: extreme injustice

The tyrannical soul represents the ultimate in human corruption. It is distinguished from the democratic type by the kinds of appetites to which it gives rein. The democrat's life was governed by a range of unnecessary desires, but the tyrant's dominant appetites fall into a special category, that of 'lawlessness' (571b). From Plato's descriptions (571c–d), these desires are largely of a grotesque sexual nature, though they also include certain violent fantasies, and extreme forms of gluttony. The tyrannical man is governed by these urges to the extent that he jettisons any other interests; his lawless appetite 'finds any beliefs or desires in the man that are thought to be good [. . .], destroys them and throws them out, until it's purged him of moderation and filled him with imported madness' (573b). His state of mind is thus, effectively, one of criminal insanity.

It is significant within the *Republic*'s argument that Socrates applies the 'tyrannical' label to the life he deems the most unjust – and moreover the most unhappy – known to man. In Book I, when Socrates debated with Thrasymachus about the value of justice, the latter spoke of a tyrant as the epitome of both injustice and supreme happiness, able to appropriate all the possessions and servants he needs to satisfy his extreme desires (344a–c). Note that Gyges, too, used the power of his magic ring to become a tyrant ruler. By presenting the tyrannical character as the most miserable and unenviable of all, Socrates thus seeks a complete inversion of his opponents' position. Far from producing the happiest of individuals, tyranny, the ultimate injustice, is a recipe for personal misery and spiritual ruin.

Socrates describes the tyrannical man, whose soul is governed by lawless appetite, as suffering in a number of ways. First, he is friendless (575e–576a). His psychology renders him incapable of entering into any human relationship, other than for the purposes of satisfying his primary impulses. Hence, whilst he might enjoy dominating people, or possibly ingratiating himself to get something out of them (for instance sexual favours), his character precludes him from engaging with anyone in a relationship of trust, equality and mutual respect. This is certainly a valid reason for finding the tyrannical life unattractive. However, it must also be noted that while *we* may value friendships of a kind which the tyrannical character cannot achieve, the tyrant himself is unlikely to regard his life as deficient on grounds of their absence. Assuming he can attain those relationships he *does* desire – ones where he can exploit others for personal gratification – he may suffer little, from his own internal perspective, from lacking relationships of the more altruistic kind.

A second claim (577c–d) is that the tyrannical individual suffers from a lack of freedom. His 'most decent parts', it is said, are 'enslaved [. . .] with a small part, the maddest and most vicious, as their master'; hence, his soul is 'least likely to do what it wants' (577d) and is 'full of disorder and regret' (577e). This is an important passage for clarifying Plato's precise conception of the tyrannical soul. It is tempting, in view of its description elsewhere as 'frenzied' and 'filled with [. . .] madness' (573b), to think of the tyrannical man as an animalistic creature, incapable of rational thought, who simply responds to whatever appetites grip him at any given moment. However, the account of him as enslaved and regretful suggests a different picture. His lack of freedom consists in his inability to do what some residual 'decent' part of him would like to, because his lawless appetite – which is immeasurably stronger – forces him in a different direction. He is perhaps rather like a drug-addict who wishes at some level to lead a normal life, but who is constantly driven by his rampant desire to consume an addictive substance. He is thus unable to do what his residual reasoning component believes is best. This account of his mindset seems necessary to assimilate Socrates' comment that he is regretful. His feeling of regret implies he is somehow capable of evaluating his own appetite-driven behaviour negatively, which would not be possible if his mind were akin to an animal's. He retains, then, a reasoning capacity of sorts, but one which is completely impotent in determining his actions.

Later in Book IX (beginning 588b), Socrates uses a metaphor for the soul in which reason is likened to a man, spirit to a lion, and appetite to a many-headed monster whose various heads represent the different appetites, some more savage and disorderly than others. In the just soul, the man will rule, making the lion his ally in taming the monster and preventing its more aggressive heads from growing too strong (589a–b). In the tyrannical soul, by contrast, we may assume the monster's most unruly heads have gained overall charge and that the man and lion are utterly powerless to prevent them from acting as they please. This metaphor further underlines the point that the tyrant is enslaved to his own baser urges: the 'beast' within. It also helps to interpret Socrates' comment, at (578a), that the tyrannical soul, like the corresponding city, is 'poor and unsatisfiable'. In the same way as a political tyrant-ruler might increasingly desire more power and resources for himself, so the lawless appetites in the tyrannical soul – the savage heads of the monster – make ever-increasing demands which it eventually becomes impossible to satisfy. As a consequence of feeding these heads by indulging in lawless pleasure, the desire for more of the same becomes so intense and frequent that it cannot always be fulfilled, leading to a permanent state of dissatisfaction as the monster grows insatiable (588e). Far from achieving fulfilment of his appetites, then, the tyrannical person augments them to such an extent that their satisfaction becomes impossible. He is never, therefore, content.

In the final stage of his reversal of Thrasymachus' eulogy to the tyrant's life, Socrates claims that the only man who is worse off than one with a tyrannical soul is one who has the additional misfortune to become an actual political tyrant (beginning 578b). On top of the various miseries outlined above, it is claimed such an individual lives in a perpetual state of fear. Realizing that his subjects resent his rule and desire his removal, possibly even his assassination, he becomes obsessed with security and unable to lead a normal life, being instead 'mostly confined to his own house' (579b). Whilst it is indeed true that many dictators have adopted a paranoid mentality of this kind – Stalin being a good example – this argument is philosophically weak as it does not necessarily hold that a political tyrant will be constantly beset by fears about his overthrow. A particularly cunning and deceitful tyrant might convince his subjects of his benevolence and hence enjoy their acclaim. A truly reckless tyrant may realize that he is unpopular but simply not care, living solely for the pleasure of the moment. Hence, while Socrates is right to point out the potential drawbacks of holding absolute political power, his argument may not be sufficient to convince those of Thrasymachus' ilk that such a life is essentially and necessarily unpleasant.

As regards Plato's general argument for the undesirability of the tyrannical soul, one might object that he selects too easy a target for this attack on injustice. Admittedly, few if any would desire their lawless appetites to run riot in their souls, such that they lose all rational control of their own lives. However, Plato's opponents – advocates of injustice – might respond that this is not the picture of the supremely unjust person they have in mind. Rather, the person they consider happy is one who makes a carefully considered choice to live for personal pleasure and who is able to achieve his ends, coolly and clinically, by the ill-use and exploitation of others. The happy man, in other words, is not one enslaved to appetite, but instead someone who chooses, rationally, to make appetite-satisfaction his life's work, and who is ruthless and successful in its accomplishment. This case of a 'rational hedonist', already raised in section 3.6.3 of this book, notably does not feature in Plato's taxonomy of characters.

At (580a–c), Socrates relates his account of the tyrant's unhappiness to his main project: the answer to Glaucon's challenge. 'Hire a herald', he triumphantly exclaims at (580b), for he believes he has demonstrated that the least just person is also the most unhappy; correspondingly, the most just, whose soul is in the best order, is the happiest. As for the intermediate souls, their happiness is ranked according to their distance from justice; the further away, the more miserable. Timocrats, then, are happier than oligarchs, who are in turn happier than democrats, with tyrants last in line.

3.11.2. The pleasures of justice and injustice

Socrates does offer two further arguments, spanning much of the remainder of Book IX, whose purpose is specifically to show that the just man's life is more *pleasant* than the unjust. Both arguments draw on a distinction, made at (580c–d), between the pleasures associated with the reasoning part of the soul (learning and philosophizing), those of the spirit (victory and honour) and those of appetite (wealth and sensuality). The first category of pleasures is the preserve of the just individual, who lives in accordance with reason and pursues correspondingly intellectual ends. In Socrates' view, these pleasures are greater and more 'true' (585e) than those pertaining to the other faculties.

His first argument (581c–583b) asks us to compare a philosopher, who is rational and just, with those whose lives are dedicated to honour (presumably timocrats) or profit (oligarchs). The philosopher, Socrates argues, is the only one with experience of all three types of pleasures, since the other two are unable to access (at least) the pleasures of the intellect (582b–c). Moreover, out of the three of them, the philosopher clearly has the best faculties of judgement (582d). His assessment of which type of pleasure is 'most pleasant' (582e), therefore, is by far the most likely to be authoritative. And it is clear from the life he chooses for himself, Socrates claims, that he views the intellectual pleasures as the strongest; as for the others, he is likely to rank the pleasures of honour above those of material wealth (583a). Hence, since the person deemed the most competent judge (i.e. the most experienced and skilful) regards the pleasures associated with justice and rationality as the greatest ones, we may take this as further 'proof' (583b) that such a life is the most intrinsically desirable.

This argument is interesting, but open to a number of criticisms. First, one might doubt Socrates' assumption, presumably based on empirical observation, that anyone experienced in the full range of pleasures – intellectual, spirited and appetitive – will necessarily judge the first to be the most pleasant. Moreover, if, as Socrates insists, the person chosen as the judge is a philosopher who has dedicated his entire life to learning, a critic might argue that he is perhaps not adequately familiar with the pleasures of the senses to make a fully informed judgement about them. While his intellectual sensibilities may be well developed, his palate or musculature might not, in which case his dismissal of gastronomic or athletic pleasures may be criticized as issuing from insufficient experience of the relevant sensations. Furthermore, as Cross and Woozley argue,[68] the fact that a rationally-orientated person regards intellectual pleasures as the most pleasant *for himself* does not necessarily imply that he finds them more pleasant than someone of the spirited or appetitive kind may find *their* preferred enjoyments. In other words, the assessment of the amount of pleasure taken in an activity seems essentially subjective and it is conceivable that some people, who are ignorant of the pleasures of the intellect, nonetheless find a greater enjoyment in sensual pleasure than the more intellectual among us derive from learning and doing philosophy.

Socrates' second argument for the superiority of the rational man's pleasures (583b–587b) is actually a conflation of two different points, each of which aims to show that the pleasures of the senses are less 'true' than those of the intellect. The initial reason given for this is that, unlike intellectual enjoyment, sensory satisfaction issues merely from the relief of some pre-existing pain, a relief which is mistaken for pleasure itself (583c–584a). Socrates' example is of someone who is cured of a physical illness, who believes this process is immensely pleasant, when it is in fact no more than the cessation of certain painful experiences (583c–d). It is easy to see how similar accounts might be given of the satisfaction of hunger, thirst or sexual desire.

This point is again problematic, as Socrates himself seems to acknowledge that not all physical pleasures can be analysed as mere pain relief. The pleasures of smell, he claims, are 'good examples' of pleasures which 'suddenly become very intense without being preceded by pain' (584b). Moreover, he fails to recognize that certain intellectual enjoyments, in which the rational person might indulge, could equally well be interpreted as involving relief of a prior condition which is painful. The experience of solving a mathematical conundrum that has long been frustrating and vexatious might be a case in point. The argument, then, that sensual pleasure alone is of dubious status, because of its association with relieving pain, is not particularly persuasive.

Socrates later appears to change his line of argument (585b) to propose another reason why sensory pleasures are less 'true' than those of philosophy. The objects of the former pleasures, which are physical (food, drink etc.), are said to 'participate [. . .] in truth' and 'in being' (585c) less than the objects of philosophic enjoyment – which are presumably, though this is not explicitly stated, the Forms. Hence, since the intellectual pleasures involve 'filling' our souls with Forms, 'things that are *more*' (585d, my italics) i.e. more true and real, while physical pleasures fill us with the less true, less real objects of sense perception, it follows according to Socrates that the former pleasures are 'really and truly [. . .] more true' (585e) than the latter. In order for this argument to convince, one must first accept Plato's radical ontology, which claims that the realm of Forms has a higher degree of reality than that perceived by the senses. Even if one grants him this, however, as Cross and Woozley argue,[69] it does not follow from the fact that a pleasure has an unreal object that the reality of the pleasure itself is diminished. We might, for example, take pleasure in something that is indisputably fiction, such as a fantasy or daydream, but this surely does not mean that our *pleasure* is also fictional. Socrates' claim that certain pleasures are less real due to the unreality of their objects seems, therefore, fallacious.

Discussion questions:

(a) Evaluate Socrates' model of the very worst kind of human character.

(b) What reasons might we have for believing that some pleasures are better than others?

(c) Overall, how successfully does Socrates answer the challenge he is set in Book II?

3.12. BOOK X – TWO FURTHER DISCOURSES (595a–621d)

Often regarded as an appendix to the main body of the *Republic*, Book X comprises discussions of two somewhat disjointed topics: first, a critique of the arts of poetry and painting (595a–608b); and second, an addendum to the defence of justice, largely focused on the immortality of the soul and the afterlife (608b–621d).

3.12.1. The critique of art

At (595b), Socrates refers back to his earlier discussion of the arts in the specific context of the guardians' education, which overlapped in Books II and III. Significantly, his discussion in Book X has a broader focus, concerning the sorts of artistic practice that should be allowed in the city as a whole, not merely in its pedagogical institutions. There is a notable hardening of Plato's line against art between the two passages where he addresses it. In Books II–III, he was willing to permit the young guardians to study some poetry and music, provided that the poetry was mostly non-imitative, or involved imitating only good characters. Book X begins, by contrast, with Socrates claiming that it is now 'even clearer [. . .] that (imitative) poetry should be altogether excluded' (595a) from the ideal city. Whilst this does not necessarily mean that *all* poetry is to be banned, Book X's proposals are more draconian than Socrates' earlier ones, not least because they seemingly apply to all classes of citizen.

The *Republic*'s two sections on the arts are similar insofar as each levels two kinds of criticism at art in general and poetry in particular. The first criticism, in either case, is epistemological: arts, it is claimed, mislead us about certain matters of fact, and artists are therefore deceivers. The second is more specifically ethical: exposure to art (and especially poetry) can lead to the corruption of human character. The framing of these objections, however, varies between the two passages, with Book X using philosophical ideas developed in the course of the *Republic*, and relying less on quoted examples from contemporary poems.

Book X begins with an epistemological critique of art (596a) using an example from painting. When a craftsman – a carpenter – makes a bed, he 'looks towards the appropriate Form', that is the Form of Bed, and the physical item of furniture he constructs is modelled on this Form. By contrast, when a painter paints a picture of a bed, what he produces is merely an imitation of the carpenter's physical bed, leading Socrates to claim that his product is 'third from the natural one' (597e). In other words, while the artist imitates what the carpenter has made, the latter is itself the mere likeness of a Form, meaning that the 'bed' created in art is twice removed from what Plato regards as the 'being' of a bed (597c) – the abstract Idea existing in the realm of Forms.

Plato's application of the theory of Forms in this passage is rather problematic when juxtaposed with his arguments in Book V, for there he claimed that only philosophers have any knowledge of Forms. In Book X, by contrast, carpenters are said to refer to the Form of Bed when constructing the apposite item. Overlooking this textual inconsistency, we might question how Plato moves from establishing that a painting of a bed is a likeness rather than a real bed (or an even more real Form), to the view (598c) that the painting is deceptive. After all, the majority of paintings are not meant to fool their viewers into believing that the objects depicted exist in reality. There is admittedly a technique known as *trompe l'oeil* painting where this is intended, but there is no indication that Plato's remarks about visual artists being deceivers are limited to this somewhat marginal case.

In order to grasp Plato's point, we should consider Socrates' line of questioning beginning at (597a). He asks Glaucon whether a painter seeks to imitate objects 'as they are, or as they appear', to which Glaucon's (eventual) answer is that he imitates only the appearance. The artist provides his own impression of the properties an object has, an impression that may well be misconceived. Socrates adjusts his example to speak of someone who paints, not the objects of craftsmanship, but craftsmen themselves: 'a painter can paint [. . .] a carpenter, or any other craftsmen, even though he knows nothing about these crafts' (598b–c). Moreover, 'if he is a good painter and displays his painting of a carpenter at a distance, he can deceive children and foolish people into thinking that it is truly a carpenter' (598c). There are two ways of understanding this passage. The most obvious is that the children and fools see the painting and believe there is an actual carpenter present – in other words, the painting is of the *trompe l'oeil* variety. However, a subtler and more common form of deception is that the painting implants in its viewers a false impression of what the work of carpentry is like. In short, the painting might deceive, not because it leads us to mistake a picture of 'X' for 'X' itself, but because it is founded on the artist's misconceptions of the nature of the objects or activities represented.

Socrates moves on from painting to argue that the poets' tendencies to write on subjects they know nothing about, and thereby give false impressions to their audiences, are of greater concern (598d). This is particularly so since, in Athenian society, poetic writers such as Homer were credited with wisdom on moral and religious matters, and their writings were used to educate and advise on such issues (see 598d–e). Socrates gave numerous examples in Book II of how contemporary poetry portrayed gods and heroes in ways which, he believed, distorted the true nature of divinity and heroism, thus misrepresenting that most important subject, the nature of goodness and virtue.[70] If poets are ignorant of such qualities, however, why are they not recognized as such? Socrates' view is that their audiences are blinded by their linguistic style and eloquence: many people believe what a poet says because of the enticing and impressive way he expresses his ideas (601a). Poetry is especially dangerous, therefore, insofar as it combines falsity of content with a considerable capacity to persuade.

There are various lines of response to Socrates' epistemological objections to poetry and painting. One is to point out that many instances of these arts do not seek to propagate knowledge, but simply to provide pleasure, for example through beauty (of physical form or language), entertainment or emotional arousal. Another reply to Socrates would be to say that some artists – the greatest in their fields – can indeed communicate important truths through their artistic media. Indeed, with respect to literary art in particular, one might contend that some works have the capacity to inform us, not only with respect to earthly Particulars, but even about the Forms. Aristotle, Plato's pupil, praises poetry for its capacity to shed light on 'universals' (*Poetics*, Book IX, 1451b6). By presenting narratives about the interactions of specific characters, a poem can pronounce on human nature, predicting, as Aristotle says, 'what such or such a kind of man will probably or necessarily say or do' (1451b8–9). This leads him to claim that poetry is 'something more philosophic and of graver import than history' (1451b5–6). Whereas history recounts only specific events which have occurred, narrative poetry seeks to analyse general truths about the human condition through the description of events in specially constructed hypothetical scenarios.

Shakespeare's *Othello*, for example, could be taken to inform us not only about one (fictional) man's jealousy, but also, more significantly, about the nature of jealousy *per se*. Viewed in this way, a literary work's project might be similar to that of philosophy, namely to analyse concepts with a view to improving our understanding of them; or in Plato's terms, to discover the nature of certain Forms.

Plato admittedly might respond that just because certain artists *seek* to offer accounts of Forms, it does not follow that their accounts are correct. Indeed, he could claim that they *cannot* be correct, as poets are not trained philosophers, and only philosophy can issue in this sort of conceptual knowledge. Hence, contrary to popular Athenian belief, the student of human nature, virtue or happiness would be far better advised to consult moral philosophers such as Socrates than poets like Homer. Indeed, it is likely that Plato's harsh invective against this poet in particular, both in Book X (598e–600e) and in Books II–III, stems from his frustration that while his own mentor was rejected and punished by his society, Homer was widely revered as 'the poet who educated Greece' (606e).

There is one other argument in Book X for why artists tend to lack knowledge of their subjects (601c–602a). The person who uses an object – say, a flute or horse-bridle – generally knows how this object should be, i.e. its ideal specifications. Equally, one whose job is to *make* the relevant object, a craftsman, will be told these specifications, for once the object is made he is held responsible for its proper functioning. But a painter, who simply imitates a flute or horse-bridle in a picture, is under no requirement to ensure that his image has the correct features of the relevant object. Unlike the craftsman who makes horse-bridles, the artist has no reason to consult with those who know how bridles should be constructed; nothing, in other words, motivates him to seek the truth about them as a basis for his work. Artists are therefore in positions of irresponsibility. There are no requirements for them to seek accurate accounts of the objects they imitate, and consequently, they tend to be ignorant of these objects, and infect their audiences with the same misconceived views. Whilst this problem may be relatively insignificant in the context of misleading pictures of horse-bridles, it is far more serious when an artist produces faulty depictions of human beings, or indeed the nature of human virtue.

This last point leads naturally on to Plato's second criticism of the arts: their tendency to corrupt human character. The ethical criticism in Book X makes specific appeal to the tripartite account of the soul from Book IV. This theme is introduced at (602c), when Socrates asks 'on which of a person's parts does [art] exert its power?' His answer is that it seeks to exploit a 'weakness in our nature' (602c–d). He substantiates this view first with respect to painting: a *trompe-l'oeil* picture induces us to believe that the depicted object is real, even though we know, rationally, that this is not so. The artwork thus produces in us an optical illusion that conflicts with our rational judgement. In this sense, Socrates suggests, it opposes and undermines reason, the 'best part of the soul' (603a).

The charge of appealing to the non-rational elements of human nature is, again, more serious when levelled at poetic literature (beginning 603b). In this case, Socrates argues that contact with poetry undermines reason by strengthening either or both of the soul's lower faculties: spirit and appetite. His argument runs thus. First, the type of human being most commonly portrayed in poetry is one who is highly emotional, 'excitable' and 'multicoloured' (604d–605a). A typical tragic hero, for example, has strong passions, is open about his feelings, given to outpourings of grief, joy, anger and so on. Such a character is publicly entertaining in ways that a rational, quiet and stable person is not (604e); hence contemporary poetry, which was written for public performance, is full of passionate heroes. When an audience witnesses the depiction of a character's emotions on stage, they are encouraged to be equally emotional in response. For example, when a hero makes a 'long lamenting speech', it is difficult to avoid sympathizing or pitying him (605d). This, however, is irrational, in Socrates' view, for the 'reasonable' reaction to a display of anguish is to consider it 'unworthy and shameful' (605e). Socrates also identifies a longer-term danger in allowing oneself to grieve in sympathy with fictional characters, namely that one is liable to transfer these responses into real-life situations. Emotional reactions to literature feed and strengthen our sentiments so that, for instance, we come to respond to our own difficulties by wallowing in self-pity and grief (606b), rather than employing 'the very thing we need', namely rational deliberation (604c).

Pity is not the only element of the soul's 'lower' regions that poetry might stimulate. Socrates also attacks comic poets for encouraging us to take pleasure in jokes that we should rightly be 'ashamed to tell' (606c). He also briefly mentions sexual desire and anger as psychological states that are nurtured by certain kinds of literature

(606d). In all these cases, the crux of the ethical criticism is the same: by engaging elements of spirit and appetite, poetry increases these faculties' strength and augments their capacity to overpower reason, thereby thwarting our development as just individuals.

How might poetry be defended against these accusations? An interesting line of opposition, again, is taken by Aristotle, who speaks of our emotional responses to art not as strengthening our emotions, but rather as bringing about their *catharsis* (*Poetics* VI, 1449b28). This word can be translated as 'purging'. The idea is that emotions such as pity and fear, which Aristotle agrees can be damaging when they occur in real-life scenarios, nonetheless require some outlet, lest they build up within us and become ever more powerful. By feeling them in response to theatrical performances – a relatively harmless context – we purge or release them from our souls, so that they are less liable to recur when we are faced with actual misfortune or danger. Taking, then, Plato's point that feeling self-pity in response to our troubles prevents our deliberating rationally about how to overcome them (604c), Aristotle might counter that someone who regularly 'lets out' his pity at the theatre is less, rather than more, likely to fall victim to this troublesome emotion in circumstances where its absence is vital. A similar point could be made about sexual desire and erotic literature. One might contend that if the sexual urge demands satisfaction one way or another, then allowing it to occur in response to literary fiction – giving vent to one's appetite – makes one less disposed to act lustfully in real situations.

These examples are, of course, open to dispute. Some might suggest that far from lessening the incidence of unwanted sexual desires, regular contact with erotic fiction renders the sexual urge all the more powerful. Equally, Plato might insist that feeling pity in response to tragedy does not purge this emotional disposition, but strengthens it, so that the feeling occurs more readily, more often and with greater intensity than it otherwise would. Ultimately, the question of which view is correct – whether emotional arousal by art increases or decreases the incidence of emotions *per se* – is probably one for empirical rather than theoretic investigation, and the answer might well differ depending on which emotion we are dealing with. The conflict between Plato and Aristotle over this matter, however, is a fascinating historical instantiation of a debate which is still relevant to modern-day discussions of censorship and the impact of art on human psychology.

There is another, quite different, reply to Plato's argument that literary art strengthens spirit and appetite, which is to say that this depends on the type of literature in question. Again, the author whom Plato has most in his sights is Homer, whose works are highly melodramatic and designed to induce emotive responses; they also frequently portray supposedly heroic characters undergoing emotional turmoil. But we might wonder how Plato would respond to a different kind of literature; one which actively promoted the life of reason, perhaps by showing rational, self-controlled heroes triumphing over villains who are dominated by appetite. One literary classic which might accomplish this end is Bram Stoker's *Dracula*, in which the arch-rationalist Professor Van Helsing ultimately wins out over the dark, passionate, erotically-connoted Count.

Indeed, there is evidence in *Republic* X that Plato himself recognizes that certain kinds of artistic writing need not be ethically corrupting. He does not propose a blanket ban on all poetry, but is willing to admit 'hymns to the gods and eulogies to good people' (607a) for public consumption. Moreover, he will allow any other poetry that 'proves it ought to have a place in a well-governed city' (607c), perhaps leaving the door open to literature that avoids excessive sentimentality or, even better, explicitly promotes rational conduct. That said, Plato's prescriptions for the poetic arts are highly illiberal by most standards, and certainly would have been viewed this way in Athens, where the vast majority of popular and acclaimed poetry would have been outlawed under his proposals. No doubt, however, he would have responded that Athenian permissiveness towards art was among the society's failings, and evidence of its characteristically 'democratic' tendency to overvalue freedom at the expense of promoting civic virtue.

3.12.2. The consequences of justice

The final pages of the *Republic* return to its main question: why is it in our interest to be just? In Books IV and IX, Socrates made his case that the possession of a just soul is intrinsically preferable to an unjust one in terms of the well-being, and indeed the pleasure, associated with each. Hence, even if, as Glaucon and Adeimantus suggested in Book II, a truly just person suffers all the penalties of a reputation for injustice, and an unjust one receives all the earthly and divine rewards normally earmarked for the virtuous, the former still has the better life on account of the underlying state of his soul. Socrates' last project in Book X is to argue that the assumptions made by the brothers in setting out their challenge are, in fact, unlikely to hold true in practice. In other words, as Socrates claims, a just person typically enjoys a range of benefits resulting from others' (humans' and gods') perceptions of his justice, whereas an unjust person pays considerable forfeits for being recognized as a villain.

Thus, Socrates argues that while unjust people might derive short-term advantages from their immoral conduct, in the end they will most likely be found out, dishonoured and punished by society (613b–614a). Likewise, it is 'generally true' (613c) that the just are recognized as such by their fellow citizens, and enjoy the worldly benefits of their good reputations. These arguments are primarily intended, it seems, to provide further incentives for Plato's readers to live justly. Their theoretical merit is questionable, however, for the punishments Socrates identifies, by his own admission, issue only contingently from unjust behaviour; he himself admits that only 'the majority' (613d) of unjust people are caught and penalized. Equally, it does not follow necessarily from one's being just that one is acknowledged and rewarded as such; this is only a 'general' relation (613c), which apparently did not hold in the case of Socrates himself. Thus, Glaucon's point that social rewards and punishments do not always attach appropriately to justice and injustice is still a perfectly valid one.

The social consequences of living justly or unjustly, while significant in themselves, are 'nothing' (614a) compared to the rewards and punishments allocated in the afterlife. In order to argue that posthumous welfare constitutes a further reason for being just, Socrates needs to establish that there is indeed an afterlife for the soul, and that it does not cease to exist with the death of the body. To this end, he offers an argument for the soul's immortality, which runs as follows (608d–611a). The destruction of any object can only be brought about, it is assumed, by the evil 'peculiar' to the object in question (609a). In the case of wood, the relevant evil is rot; with metal, it is rust; for a living body, it is sickness. Now, the peculiar evil of a human soul – the thing which 'makes it bad', in Socrates' words – is injustice, or more generally, vice (609b–c). But it is clear that being unjust or vicious does not bring about a soul's destruction; after all, people do not die as a result of their bad character (610e). Therefore, since the evil peculiar to the soul does not destroy it, and evils peculiar to other objects cannot do so by definition, it follows that the soul cannot be destroyed and is thus immortal.

This argument is unconvincing and far too cursory in its treatment of a profound topic to carry much weight.[71] The main objection to it is that insufficient justification is offered for the premise that the only evil which could possibly render a soul extinct is ethical vice. Socrates simply overlooks all other possibilities, including the eminently plausible view that being denied residence in a living body is fatal for a soul. As Annas points out,[72] Socrates assumes that the fate of the body has no bearing on the soul whatsoever, thereby implicitly committing himself to a thesis for which he offers no argument, to the effect that soul and body are distinct kinds of entity, each of which can exist without the other. In the absence of any metaphysical grounding for such a position, his assertion that the soul lives on 'even if the body is cut up into tiny pieces' (610b) is gravely unsupported.

Of course, the inadequacy of this particular argument for the soul's immortality does not prove that it is indeed mortal, or that there is no afterlife. Socrates' claim that posthumous rewards and punishments constitute reasons for being just (614a) makes a further assumption, however, namely that the nature of the afterlife is one which involves divine judgement and sanction. For this he offers no corroboration as such, but merely a lengthy anecdote (beginning 614b): the so-called 'Myth of Er'.

This is the story of a Pamphylian soldier who undergoes what we might term a 'near death' experience after being laid unconscious (presumed dead) on the battlefield. Reviving several days later, he tells the story of his journey to the next world, during which he observed how the souls of the dead are treated in the afterlife. They are, it transpires, sorted into two groups (614d): the just, who travel upwards to the heavens; and the unjust, who are sent into the bowels of the earth. Thereafter, each group undertakes a thousand-year journey, in the course of which they receive rewards or punishments proportionate to the magnitude of their deeds. The unjust suffer ten times the intensity of pain they caused their victims, ten times over during their millennium in Hades (615a–b); the just are 'rewarded according to the same scale' (615b). After the thousand-year period has elapsed, the souls are reunited prior to reincarnation, and are permitted to choose the nature of their next earthly life, be it human or animal (617d–619d). Reincarnation is denied, however, to those who have committed the worst atrocities (most of them tyrants), who are condemned to languish for eternity in the pit of Tartarus (615c–616a).

It is unclear how literally Plato intends his readers to take the Myth of Er. The story certainly provides an entertainingly poetic conclusion to the *Republic* as a whole, and offers yet another incentive for justice (together with an especially strong disincentive for tyranny). One must remember, however, that unlike many moral educators both in his own society and subsequently, Plato is not reliant on descriptions of the afterlife to explain why being just is to an agent's personal advantage. He has already shown this, as he believes, by his accounts of the soul's welfare in *this* world, let alone the next.

Discussion questions:
(a) Do the arts help us or hinder us in the control of our emotions?
(b) Is there any good reason for believing in the existence of an afterlife?

CHAPTER 4

RECEPTION AND INFLUENCE

Such is the wide range of subjects and arguments dealt with in the *Republic*, and so open is its content to differences of interpretation, that it is impossible to provide a full catalogue of its influence on subsequent philosophies and social trends. In this chapter I shall therefore confine myself to three circumscribed projects. The first is to examine how Plato's own student, Aristotle, responded to the *Republic*, criticizing certain elements but developing and expanding others and using them as stimuli for his own ideas. The second considers the relationship between the political theories espoused in the *Republic* and the political practice of the twentieth and twenty-first centuries, evaluating the relevance of Plato's work to liberal-democratic societies and their recent ideological opponents. The third subsection looks briefly at the modern-day impact of Plato's contributions to ethics and moral psychology.

4.1. ARISTOTLE'S REACTION

It was noted in section 3.12.1 how Aristotle's discussions of tragedy in his *Poetics* seem to contain implicit criticisms of Plato's treatment of poetry and the arts. This, however, is just one of a number of passages in Aristotle which engage, explicitly or otherwise, with different aspects of the *Republic*.

4.1.1. Political theory

The most direct response to the work is found in Aristotle's *Politics*, where the first five chapters of Book II constitute a critique of the political system Plato advocates, primarily his proposals for the abolition of families and private property among the guardian class. These policies, Aristotle argues, are founded on Plato's desire to make the ideal state 'as unified as possible' (1261a15); a misguided goal according to Aristotle, as he believes a state is more likely to achieve 'self-sufficiency' the greater the diversity among its people (1261b14–15). Even granted Plato's assumption that unity is the most valuable of political ends, however, Aristotle believes it unlikely to be achieved through the measures put forward in the *Republic*. First, the removal of family ties will not, as Plato maintains, lead to the guardians extending the concern we normally reserve for our family to the entire class. Rather, it will lead to a universal neglect of others (1262a1–2); the feelings of love and affection generally associated with kinship will become 'diluted' (1262b15), as there is 'no reason why the so-called father should care about the son, or the son about the father' (1262b20–1).

Second, denying the guardians rights to property will not result in the fraternity Plato is seeking, but rather in 'a world of trouble' (1263a11) between those who are asked to share land and income due to disagreements over their relative deserts. Aristotle contends that Plato's opposition to private property overlooks an inherent, natural selfishness in human nature, which leads people to derive pleasure from ownership (1263a40ff.); something the guardians in Plato's ideal state are not allowed. The fact that they own nothing also denies them, on Aristotle's account, the opportunity to exhibit the virtue of liberality by using their possessions for the good of others (1263a10ff.).

Book II, Chapter 5 of the *Politics* concludes with several more general objections to the political arrangements recommended in the *Republic*. Aristotle mounts an archetypal 'conservative' argument to the effect that Plato's proposed radical reforms ignore the 'experience of ages' (1263b42ff.); in other words, if the system he advocates is likely to work in practice and have the benefits he outlines, surely it would have been discovered, and experimented with, already? This general point is followed by a rather summary rejection of the proposal that women should engage in the same occupations as men, on grounds that this would leave the task of 'household management' unattended (1264b4ff). It is evident from Book I of the *Politics* that Aristotle holds a far more conventional opinion than Plato concerning the function of women in society, claiming their natural role is to be subservient to men (see 1259b3,

1260a22–3). On the other hand, Aristotle also condemns the lack of social mobility within Plato's ideal system. Applying the 'myth of the metals' will inevitably lead, he argues, to a situation where 'the same persons' (1264b9) – the 'golden' souls born into the guardian class – are invariably appointed as rulers. Aristotle's critique of the *Republic* ends by questioning what is meant by deeming it the guardians' duty to make 'the whole city' happy.[1] It makes little sense to speak of the happiness of a state as a whole, he suggests, independently of the happiness of its parts; that is, the individual citizens which constitute it (1264b15ff.).[2]

4.1.2. Ethics, psychology and the Forms

Although Aristotle's response to the *Republic*'s political theory is largely critical, much of its material on ethics and moral psychology had a profound influence on his own work. In the *Nicomachean Ethics* (hereafter referred to as *NE*), Aristotle's most famous treatise on virtue and happiness, he follows Plato in postulating significant connections between (a) being happy (achieving *eudaimonia*); (b) possessing the moral virtues, including justice; and (c) thinking and acting in accordance with reason. The main argument of the *Republic* is that the happiest life is the just one; and being just, on Plato's view, means that reason is predominant within one's soul. Book I of Aristotle's *NE* also addresses the nature of happiness, and here Aristotle argues that one is happy insofar as one fulfils one's function (*ergon*), which involves doing whatever is characteristically associated with one's nature, i.e. peculiar to the type of being that one is (1097b22ff.). In the case of man, his nature is to exercise reason, since this is the faculty that sets him apart from the remainder of the animal kingdom and other inanimate objects. Thus, the characteristic activity of man, on Aristotle's view, is 'an activity of soul in accordance with, or not without, rational principle' (1098a7–8). And since happiness consists in performing one's characteristic activity, the happy life for man must involve the exercise of his rational faculties.

Aristotle adds, moreover, that his account of happiness is in harmony with 'those who identify happiness with virtue' (1098b30, the Greek term for virtue is *aretē*, also sometimes translated as 'excellence'). He thus implies, along similar lines to Plato, that a happy life – which on his account involves rationality – is also a virtuous one. Several passages of the *NE* suggest specific links between the use of reason and moral virtue. The virtuous person is said to exercise 'practical wisdom' (*phronēsis*) in correctly determining what it is best to do in any given situation (see 1107a1–2, 1144b21–8); and this is a quality of the intellect (1103a6). In a virtuous soul, moreover, the emotions and appetites are said to 'speak with the same voice as reason' (1102b28), rather than motivating actions contrary to reason's judgements. This reflects the Platonic account of the just man, whose passions are controlled by his rational element.

Aristotle's analysis of reason itself, however, is more sophisticated than Plato's. He draws a division between theoretic reason, such as is exercised in philosophy and other academic disciplines, and practical reason, which is employed when rationally determining how to act, and which, like the rational element of Plato's tripartite soul, can motivate action in and of itself (1139a35). This distinction is not evident in the *Republic*. Indeed, Plato seemingly holds that the development of theoretical reason automatically brings practical rationality in its wake. This is implied, particularly, by his account of the philosopher-ruler, whose theoretical knowledge of the Form of the Good enables him to govern the state efficiently in practice. Aristotle's distinction between the practical and the theoretic, however, is a plausible basis for criticism of this Platonic view. The fact that a philosopher understands the nature of goodness in the abstract, Aristotle could argue, does not necessarily enable him to ensure the good of the state, as he may be insufficiently skilled in practicalities of policy-making.

The distinction between two types of reason also produces an ambiguity in Aristotle's account of happiness, which relates to questions arising from the *Republic*. While most of the *NE* implies that the happy (*eudaimōn*) life is one of active virtue, involving exercise of practical reason, its final book (Book X) suggests that since the intellect is 'the best thing in us' (1177a20–1), the contemplative life of a theoretician might be happier still. Indeed, such a life is deemed 'divine' in comparison with ordinary human existence (1177b31ff.), though it is still something for which human beings may reasonably strive. In the *Republic*, the notion that a trained philosopher might prefer to contemplate the Forms rather than be involved in practical politics, and thus feel unfulfilled in his role as a guardian, was implied in the metaphor of the 'return to the cave', but never developed in detail. We might, however, interpret

Aristotle's presentation of two different accounts of *eudaimonia* as highlighting a dilemma to which Plato merely alluded; namely, whether the best life to pursue is really one of practical good works and engagement with one's fellow men, or whether someone may achieve a higher order of happiness by devoting himself to private intellectual study.

Turning to the non-rational parts of the human soul, Aristotle's accounts of these again owe much to Plato's, though they are more sophisticated. He seems, in places, to accept Plato's distinction between *thumos* and *epithumia*, sometimes speaking of anger and appetite as different types of human faculty (see 1111b13) and in one passage suggesting that the former is more likely to obey reason than the latter (1149a26ff.). This reflects Plato's idea that while spirit can potentially become reason's ally, appetite is more unruly and must be kept firmly in check. Aristotle offers a more complex picture, however, of the range of non-rational elements within the human psyche. Moving beyond the simple division between spirit and appetite, which, as argued in section 3.6.1, seems not to exhaust all possible emotional states, Aristotle distinguishes a wider range of non-rational feelings (*pathē*) which can motivate action. Besides anger and attraction to sensory pleasure, these include fear and confidence, pride and humility, friendly feeling, envy and spite. He provides a detailed taxonomy of emotions in the *Rhetoric* (1378a21ff.); and in *NE* Books III and IV he classifies the full range of human virtues, suggesting that each is associated with a different emotional phenomenon (courage is linked to fear and confidence; temperance to the sensory appetites, and so on).

Another feature of the *Republic* with which Aristotle engages in some detail is the theory of Forms. He devotes *NE* Book I, Chapter 6, to a critique of Plato's account of the Form of the Good – a notion about which he is sceptical, for several reasons. He argues, for example, that the various things we deem 'good' do not share any common property which links them all to the same Form (1096b21ff.). Moreover, he questions the claim that one might use one's knowledge of the Form of Goodness as a model for pursuing good outcomes in a given practical sphere, a view which is central to Plato's account of how the philosopher-ruler operates. According to Aristotle, practitioners in particular crafts, such as weavers, generals and doctors, who seek to achieve good outcomes in their designated fields, are not assisted in doing so by reference to abstract ideals

(1097a7ff.). Rather, they require knowledge of how to achieve specific goods associated with particular events and objects; the health of a given patient, for instance, in a medic's case. Extending this argument, we might doubt whether political power is, as Plato believes, best wielded by those who understand goodness in purely theoretical terms. Following Aristotle, we might perhaps prefer as rulers those with hands-on experience of public affairs who are experts in the specific practical issues and institutions concerned.[3] Again, while Plato's approach to politics is essentially ideological, seeking to model the city on abstract conceptions of virtue and the Good, Aristotle's is more pragmatic, aiming to achieve piecemeal ends through the exercise of practical good sense.

4.2. THE *REPUBLIC* AND MODERN POLITICS

The status of the political passages of the *Republic* is uncertain, partly because it may be questioned how much of Plato's account of the just state he genuinely intends as proposals for political reform. After all, Socrates' original reason for introducing the *polis* in Book III was to demonstrate by analogy why it is better for an individual soul to be just than unjust. It is therefore possible, on one reading, to take the description of the ideal state primarily as a metaphorical device for illustrating the nature and benefits of justice as a virtue of character. On the other hand, the detail Plato offers concerning civic arrangements – for instance with respect to the rulers' education, the status of women and childrearing – suggest that he did mean to intertwine significant political views with his ethical theory. This book has therefore sought to engage as seriously as possible with the former as well as the latter.

Even granted such an approach, the present-day reader might wonder how much relevance the *Republic*'s political ideas have to the politics of contemporary Western societies, which are organized along liberal-democratic lines very different from those advocated by Plato. Indeed, as was noted in section 3.5.3, some of Plato's sternest critics are committed liberal thinkers such as Karl Popper. This section will outline some of the major differences between Plato's ideals and the democratic realities of the modern-day Western world. It will also identify, however, certain elements of Plato's thought which have been, or might still be, influential in efforts to mould our political institutions. Lastly, it will evaluate possible connections between Plato's proposals and two of the most significant anti-democratic ideologies of the twentieth century, communism and fascism.

4.2.1. Liberal democracy

Popper levels a plethora of objections at Plato. He accuses him of promoting a strict division of social classes – effectively a 'caste' system[4] – in which the minority in the higher classes enjoy a monopoly of academic and military education.[5] 'Knowing one's place' in society, and indeed willingly accepting it, are praised as hallmarks of the good citizen; indeed, the political virtues of justice and moderation are defined in precisely these terms.[6] Propaganda is used to maintain the status quo, while innovation and individual liberty are rigorously suppressed.[7] In general, Popper claims, Plato regards it as the task and purpose of each individual to promote the stability of the state, rendering the state's interests the ultimate criterion of personal morality.[8] Such a view might potentially be used to justify the state ill-treating or even doing violence to its citizens in order to maximize its own well-being.

As discussed in section 3.5.3, there is room for disagreement over the extent of Plato's 'totalitarianism'.[9] Nowhere does he say explicitly that it is acceptable to ignore individual interests to benefit the whole state, and in the passage where he comes closest to doing so (420b–421c), it is the ruling class, and not the majority, whose interests seem to be overlooked, as they must be cajoled into performing their governmental duties. It is undeniable, however, that Plato assigns little, or even a negative, value to individual liberty, which he associates with democracy, the second-worst political system according to the ranking in *Republic* VIII. His main reason for limiting freedom is his lack of faith in the majority of citizens. They are incapable, he believes, of making sound rational judgements of how to conduct their lives, and should therefore submit to the rules laid down by the knowledgeable guardians (431b–d).

The modern Western world generally takes a less paternalistic view of the role of government. John Stuart Mill, in the nineteenth century,[10] argued that adults should be free from governmental interference to make decisions concerning their own lives, provided they do not harm others; a view which has been highly influential in modern liberal societies. Even if some people make mistaken judgements, it is generally thought better that they are free to choose wrongly instead of being forced to do what is in their 'best interest', which would deny them autonomy, perhaps the most important liberal value. There are admittedly exceptions to this: laws concerning the wearing of seatbelts and drug-taking are largely aimed at protecting people against their own folly, something of which Plato might have approved. He would perhaps have been less supportive of the modern-day concern for privacy. Liberal societies generally advocate the existence of a private sphere in which individuals' activities are not subject to state intrusion. There is no mention of this in the *Republic*, and indeed the proposals for the guardians' lifestyles deny them the privacy associated with family life and property, which are nowadays regarded as basic human rights.

The other main liberal charge against Plato concerns his division of society into three classes. This, it might be claimed, locks individuals into certain roles and denies them opportunities to better themselves in terms of status, employment or education. Even Aristotle, by no means an obvious 'liberal' thinker, objected to the *Republic* on grounds that Plato's system produces a fixed ruling class, with power inaccessible to those outside it (1264b6ff.). The extent to which Plato believed one's position in society should be fixed by one's heredity, though, is open to question. Admittedly, his proposals in *Republic* V for mating rituals to breed guardians from the most able of the current generation suggest that he sees intelligence and virtue as inherited traits. However, he explicitly states in Book III that those born into lower class families can become guardians if they demonstrate sufficient ability, whilst any guardian offspring who fail to meet expectations must be demoted to the productive class (415b–c). This suggests his division of classes is meritocratic (i.e. based on aptitude) rather than being determined solely by breeding. Moreover, the fact that his proposals for women guardians are perceived by some commentators as feminist[11] further undermines allegations of extreme conservatism.

There are admittedly certain features of Plato's system which it is difficult to reconcile with the present-day concern for equality of opportunity. His educational system is devoted to the production of good rulers, and is thus limited to an intellectual elite. There is no suggestion that members of the productive class might benefit from the expansion of their minds through academic study. Citizens seem to lack any choice over their occupations, which are dictated by considerations of what best suits their abilities and training. Whether this necessarily means sacrificing their well-being for that of the state, however, is open to doubt, as one might argue that people are better off undertaking work that fits their capacities rather than attempting what is beyond them.

It might be questioned whether there is *any* element of the *Republic* which is truly reflected in Western politics today. One respect in which our institutions perhaps do acknowledge Plato's critique of the Athenian model of democracy is in the degree of participation in politics we allow to 'ordinary' members of the public. Plato believed that government is best conducted by knowledgeable experts, free from the influence of the uninformed majority. In Athens, by contrast all free male citizens, regardless of expertise, had rights to attend the Assembly, and were eligible to be chosen by lot to hold public office. The contemporary Western model of politics seeks a compromise between accounting for the broad wishes of the majority and obtaining the benefits of rule by the most able and best educated. Its democracy is thus representative rather than direct, meaning that the citizens elect leaders to represent them in legislative or executive capacities instead of voting themselves on policy matters and participating directly in institutions of state. Admittedly, referenda are used with varying frequencies in different nations; however, direct decision-making by citizens is far more limited than it was in Plato's Athens. Appointment to positions in the civil service and judiciary, moreover, are generally screened for ability and usually require high levels of training and educational achievement. Certain elements of modern democracies might, then, meet with Plato's approval, at least when compared with the radically democratic culture of his own city.

Another area of politics which concerned Plato, and has provoked fervent discussion in recent years, involves the relation between politicians' public roles and their private affairs. The British political scene in the 1990s was dominated by instances of political scandal concerning the sexual and financial conduct of Ministers, leading to several resignations and precipitating the fall of the Conservative government. In the US, similarly, Bill Clinton's second presidential term was marred by issues concerning his private life and his suitability for office. Plato was aware of the potential for private concerns involving family or finances to distract rulers from effectively pursuing the state's interests, hence his radical proposals for abolishing nuclear families and instituting common ownership among the just city's guardians. While by modern standards these measures seem highly draconian, the problem they address is nonetheless relevant to today's political scene. There might, moreover, be considerable support today for the suggestion that the business activities of politicians (for example) should be limited to minimize conflict between these private concerns and impartial fulfilment of public duties. As Plato put it, the roles of civic guardian and 'household manager' may not always be compatible (417a).

4.2.2. Communism

As the *Republic*'s political theories, for the most part, conflict with liberal democratic principles, we might consider how closely they relate to the non-democratic ideologies which competed with liberal democracy in the twentieth century. Certain elements of Plato's system can be likened to aspects of communism, as practised in the former Eastern bloc, and in contemporary Cuba. In particular, Plato's arguments for the sharing of possessions among the guardians and auxiliaries; his opposition to financial inequality on grounds that it is socially divisive (551d); and his collectivist vision of all citizens working in their optimal role for the benefit of society, are consonant with the professed aims and practices of communist states. The freeing of women from lives of domestic servitude and the abolition of family units, replacing them with state-run nurseries and crèches, are reminiscent of attempts following the Russian revolution to transcend the 'old morality' with its patriarchal overtones. Moreover, Plato's proposal for government by a trained elite, which acts in the state's best interests without being subject to democratic constraints, resembles the Politburo system employed in the former Soviet Union and other communist regimes.

There are limits, however, to the similarities between Plato's ideals and those of twentieth-century communism, whose ideological underpinnings were much more directly influenced by the works of Karl Marx. The *Republic*'s radical calls for public ownership and community of wives and children is restricted to the ruling and auxiliary classes, seemingly leaving the vast majority to operate with private possessions and traditional family structures. Likewise, there is no reference in the *Republic* to producer-class women taking on similar employment to their male counterparts.

As Crossman[12] explains, moreover, Plato differs significantly from Marx both in his diagnosis of societal problems and his proposals for change. Whereas Marxism begins with a critique of the injustices and economic inefficiencies of capitalism, Plato was more worried by the danger of the uneducated masses wielding political power. Consequently, while Marx and his disciples envisaged a new economic and political system ultimately directed by the proletariat, Plato regarded producers as incapable of political wisdom, requiring that they submit to the rule of their intellectual superiors. Communism saw revolutionary change as issuing from the workers' desires for material advancement, something which Plato might well have dismissed as the appetitive strivings of disordered souls. Finally, while Marxism ultimately sought a new world-order with the destruction of individual states, Plato regarded the well-run city as the locus of political justice.

4.2.3. Fascism

Perhaps one could argue that Plato has more in common with recent opponents of democracy on the far right than those on the Marxist left. There are certain features of his utopia which, indeed, seem to foreshadow aspects of twentieth-century fascism. These include, for example, his opposition to democracy; his strong support for a unified state without different parties or factions; and his belief in 'absolute' rule with no checks or limitations on the power of leaders to assert their will. Likewise, his proposals for using propaganda – for example circulating the 'myth of the metals' – to promote loyalty to existing institutions, and censoring works of art thought likely to corrupt the national ethos, were echoed in the policies of Hitler and his far-right allies.

On the other hand, there are again important divergences between Plato's ideology and that of the radical right. Acton[13] characterizes fascism as an anti-rationalist position: rejecting the Enlightenment notion of there being certain ends it is rational for all human beings to pursue, fascists view history as a struggle between competing cultures, the 'best' of which is simply whichever survives and manages to impose its way of life upon others. Equally, the notion of an objective morality, according to fascism, is bogus; moral arguments are nothing more than justifications or excuses for self-interested conduct by individuals or states.

These views would be strongly opposed by Plato, who believes it possible to discover the objective nature of goodness through rational investigation, and to govern in accordance with the truth about what is intrinsically valuable. Likewise, the Platonic conception of human virtue and happiness as involving the primacy of reason over the passions, and his advocacy of government by the most learned people within the state, are at odds with the fascist propagation of an emotive – even unreasoning – nationalism, their elevation of militarism, and their frequent suspicion of intellectuals. While Plato is certainly no pacifist, moreover, he does not share the fascist predilection for asserting the power of one's nation over others.[14] Such policies seem more likely to be associated with timocracy, on Plato's model (547e–548a), than with political justice.

4.3. PLATO AND CONTEMPORARY ETHICS

Ethical theories can be divided, broadly speaking, into three categories. *Consequentialist* views claim that the ethical merit of an action depends on its consequences: the most obvious example is the Utilitarian theory of Jeremy Bentham and John Stuart Mill, which holds that an action is morally right insofar as it leads to the maximization of human happiness. *Deontological* theories, by contrast, hold that moral action consists in obedience to a set of duties which must be observed regardless of the outcomes of doing so. On such accounts certain actions, such as murder, adultery or lying, may be deemed wrong whatever the circumstances, while others, such as paying debts or being loyal to friends, may be obligatory regardless of their consequences in a given situation. The most influential ethicist to propose such a view is perhaps Immanuel Kant, with his notion of the Categorical Imperative. The third species of ethical theory is known as *virtue theory*. Unlike the others, this does not focus on the rightness or wrongness of individual actions, but rather on the goodness or badness of human beings. Rather than addressing the questions 'what should be done', or 'what rule of conduct should be applied', virtue theorists consider what it means to have a good, that is, virtuous, character. The focus of their work is often, therefore, on the psychological states associated with making ethical decisions, rather than the justification of specific maxims or principles of action.

After a period of unpopularity, virtue ethics enjoyed a revival in the second half of the twentieth century, caused in part by increasing scepticism among philosophers about the viability of deontological or consequentialist theories of moral action. Elizabeth Anscombe (1958) believed that moral philosophers should leave aside questions of what one 'ought' morally to do, and focus instead on the ethical agent; addressing concepts in the philosophy of psychology, such as 'action', 'pleasure', 'intention', and 'wanting', before advancing to consider virtue itself. A number of leading late twentieth-century ethicists – among them Alisdair MacIntyre, Philippa Foot and Bernard Williams – followed this route.[15] It might be argued that the *Republic*, too, specifically promotes a virtue-theoretic approach to ethics in place of more conventional models based on rules of action. In Book I, the definitions of justice proposed by Cephalus and Polemachus are akin to a deontologist's enumeration of absolute duties; on these accounts, being just involves performing certain kinds of actions, such as truth-telling, repaying debts, or doing good to friends and harm to enemies. Such views are rejected, however, and Socrates offers an alternative definition of justice in terms of the structure of an agent's soul. According to Annas, one of the *Republic*'s main themes is this shift from focusing on what an agent must *do* in order to be just to what he must *be* – the sort of character he should acquire.[16] The discussion of moral psychology is clearly a major feature of the work; besides offering sketches of four different virtues, Plato includes a taxonomy of different character types.

Another element of *Republic*'s argument which has ongoing relevance to debates in ethics is Plato's account of the reasons for pursuing justice. The question 'why should I be moral?', raised by Thrasymachus and Glaucon in Books I and II, has continued to intrigue philosophers, and receives attention from contemporary writers such as Bernard Williams[17] and Thomas Nagel.[18] Plato's answer to the question is distinguished by his suggestion that having a just soul promotes an agent's own well-being; that is, justice benefits not only others but also oneself, insofar as it involves having a well-ordered psyche. The doctrine that an agent's own welfare is the ultimate justification for his morality has become known as *eudaimonism*, after the Greek term for happiness. This view resonates in the proverb 'virtue is its own reward', and challenges those in the modern world who regard the ultimate justifications for moral behaviour as lying in the interests of others or the demands of a deity. In particular, eudaimonism stands in stark contrast to views of moral conduct as involving sacrifice of oneself, or one's own interests, to some selfless end.

Plato's picture of the ideal human character as one dominated by reason might be opposed by many today on grounds that it overlooks the importance of emotions in the ethical life, in particular those emotions involving responses to the needs or happiness of other human beings. The Socratically just individual does what he rationally judges best in the attempt to imitate the Form of the Good. There is no mention, however, of his being motivated by compassion or feelings of love or friendship; indeed, it is hard to place such passions within Plato's tripartite model of the soul. Being drawn more to contemplation of the abstract than to interpersonal attachments, his life might lack many of the human relationships we nowadays deem valuable. The strict suppression of appetites recommended in the *Republic* might also be queried. While most people would advocate control of the violent or sadistic urges, Plato deems 'lawless' the sidelining of any sexual and gastronomic satisfactions from the account of the 'good life' may appear excessively puritanical. Indeed, following a Freudian line, we might wonder whether the rigorous control of 'animal instincts' could have negative consequences for psychological health.

A final area where Plato's views are of contemporary interest, albeit largely for their stark contrast with much modern-day thought, is in the field of meta-ethics; that is, accounts of the nature of our beliefs about morality, or *what it means* to make a moral judgement. With the decline of religious faith in many Western societies, the view that there are objective facts about right and wrong, or good and evil, has become less commonplace. Moral *subjectivism*, the view that moral statements are merely expressions of the speaker's attitudes; and moral *relativism*, the idea that moral judgements can only be justified relative to the conventions of a given society or culture, have permeated many social institutions and arguably diminished the strength of our commitments to ethical principles. Plato's position on meta-ethics is clearly opposed to these views. While rejecting traditional theism as a source of ethical truth, he holds that there are objective standards of goodness to be discovered by looking outside of ordinary human existence to the abstract realm of Forms. The metaphysics underlying such a view may be bizarre by modern standards; however, the conclusion that there are truths about ethical goodness to be discovered, if only we knew how, still holds appeal for many.

CHAPTER 5

NOTES FOR FURTHER READING

TRANSLATIONS

There are numerous English translations of the *Republic*; two of the best known date back to the turn of the nineteenth century. Benjamin Jowett's version, made in 1901, has been widely disseminated; a paperback edition was launched in 1992 by Random House Publishers (New York), and the full text is available on the Internet at classics.mit.edu/Plato. A. D. Lindsay's venerable translation, dating back to 1907, was reprinted in 1993 by J. M. Dent/Everyman (London). Another classic, albeit later, version is by F. M. Cornford (1941), available from Oxford University Press with an introduction and notes by the translator.

The post-war years witnessed a steady flow of *Republic* translations. Desmond Lee's version was first published by Penguin Books (London) in 1955, and has since been revised on several occasions for subsequent printings. In 1962 Heinemann (London) published a translation by W. Boyd, complete with editorial commentary, under the title *Plato's Republic for Today*. Grube's version, widely acclaimed for its combination of readability and faithfulness to the original Greek, first came to press in 1974; its later revision by C. D. C. Reeve, published by Hackett (Indianapolis) in 1992, is favoured by many university courses and has been used to supply the quotations for this book. Other alternatives include Allan Bloom's *The Republic of Plato*, republished in 1991 by Basic Books (New York), and Robin Waterfield's translation made available in 1998 by Oxford University Press. The Bloom version might be singled out as the most literal available, which does make for rather difficult reading.

Secondary Literature

There are several superbly detailed commentaries on the *Republic* as a whole, of which the two most frequently referenced in this book are Julia Annas' *An Introduction to Plato's Republic* (Oxford: Oxford University Press, 1981), and R. Cross and D. Woozley's *Plato's Republic: A Philosophical Commentary* (London: Macmillan, 1964). Others well worthy of attention include Nicholas White, *A Companion to Plato's Republic* (Oxford: Blackwell, 1979); C. D. C. Reeve, *Philosopher Kings* (Princeton: Princeton University Press, 1988), and chapters 11–17 of T. Irwin, *Plato's Ethics* (Oxford: Oxford University Press, 1995). Karl Popper's *The Open Society and its Enemies*, vol. 1 (London: Routledge, 1995) contains an interesting critical evaluation, with particular focus on the *Republic*'s political elements.

Several articles and sections of books relevant to aspects of the *Republic* or related philosophical topics have been referenced in Chapters 3 and 4 of this book; a bibliography is given below. There are a number of other seminal works, moreover, which are invaluable in the study of particular aspects of Plato's work. A short selection of these, corresponding to different topics, is given below.

For an historical overview of the Athenian society in which Plato lived:

Joint Association of Classical Teachers   (1984) *The World of Athens*. Cambridge: Cambridge University Press.

There are easily accessible introductions to Plato's life, works and main ideas in:

Melling, D.   (1987) *Understanding Plato*. Oxford: Oxford University Press.

Ryle, G.   (1966) *Plato's Progress*. Cambridge: Cambridge University Press.

The overall form of the argument in the *Republic* is ably considered in:

Mabbott, J. D.   (1937) 'Is Plato's Republic Utilitarian?' in G. Vlatos (ed.), *Plato: A collection of critical essays*, vol. II. New York: Anchor, 1971.

For an illuminating overview of Thrasymachus' position in Book I:

Nicholson, P.   (1974) 'Unravelling Thrasymachus' arguments in the *Republic*', in *Phronesis* 19, pp. 210–32.

On the analogy between state and soul:

Vlastos, G.   (1971) 'Justice and happiness in the Republic', in his *Plato: A collection of critical essays*, vol. II. New York: Anchor.

Williams, B.   (1973) The analogy of city and soul in the Republic', repr. in G. Fine (ed.), *Plato 2: Ethics, Politics, Religion and the Soul*. Oxford: Oxford University Press, 1999, pp. 255–64.

For further analysis of the *Republic*'s sections dealing with epistemology and metaphysics, the account of knowledge and the sun, line and cave metaphors:

Fine, G.   (1978) 'Knowledge and belief in *Republic* V', in *Archiv für Geschichte der Philosophie* 60, pp. 121–39.

Malcolm, J.   (1962) 'The line and the cave', in *Phronesis* 7, pp. 38–45.

Raven, J. E.   (1965) *Plato's Thought in the Making*. Cambridge: Cambridge University Press, Ch. 10.

Plato's critique of art and poetry is addressed in:

Murdoch, I.   (1977) *The Fire and the Sun: Why Plato Banished the Artists*. Oxford: Oxford University Press.

Nehemas, A.   (1982) 'Plato on imitation and poetry in *Republic* 10', in J. Moravcsik & P. Temko (eds), *Plato on Beauty, Wisdom and the Arts*. New Jersey: Rowman & Allanheld. (This collection contains several useful contributions on this area).

Tate, J. (1928)   'Imitation in Plato's Republic', in *Classical Quarterly* 22, pp. 16–23.

Selective Bibliography

Acton, H. B.   (1938) 'The Alleged Fascism of Plato', in *Philosophy* 13, pp. 302–12.

Annas, J.   (1981) *An Introduction to Plato's Republic*.
                   Oxford: Oxford University Press.
                   (1976) 'Plato's Republic and feminism', in
                   Philosophy, 51, pp. 307–21.
Anscombe, E.   (1958) 'Modern moral philosophy', in
                   Philosophy 33, pp. 1–19.
Cross, R. &   (1964) *Plato's Republic: A Philosophical*
Woozley, D.   *Commentary*. London: Macmillan.
Cooper, J. M.   (1984) 'Plato's theory of human moti-
                   vation', in *History of Philosophy Quarterly*,
                   pp. 3–21.
Crossman, R. H. S. (1959) *Plato Today*. London: Allen & Unwin.
Dahl, N. O.   (1995) 'Plato's defence of justice', in G. Fine
                   (ed.), *Plato 2: Ethics, Politics, Religion and the
                   Soul*. Oxford: Oxford University Press, 1999,
                   pp. 207–34.
Davidson, D.   (1980) 'How is weakness of will possible?' in his
                   Essays on Actions and Events. Oxford:
                   Clarendon Press, 1980, pp. 21–43.
Foot, P.   (1978) *Virtues and Vices*. Oxford: Blackwell.
Harrison, T. R.   (1993) *Democracy*. London: Routledge.
Kraut, R.   (1991) 'Return to the cave: *Republic* 519–521',
                   repr. in G. Fine (ed.), *Plato 2: Ethics, Politics,
                   Religion and the Soul*. Oxford: Oxford
                   University Press, 1999, pp. 235–54.
MacIntyre, A.   (1981) *After Virtue*. London: Duckworth.
Nagel, T.   (1970) *The Possibility of Altruism*. Princeton,
                   NJ: Princeton University Press.
Popper, K.   (1995) *The Open Society and its Enemies*.
                   London: Routledge (first published 1945).
Rawls, J.   (1973) *A Theory of Justice*. Oxford: Oxford
                   University Press.
Reeve, C.   (1988) *Philosopher Kings*. Princeton, NJ:
                   Princeton University Press.
Sachs, D.   (1963) 'A fallacy in Plato's *Republic*', in
                   Philosophical Review 72, pp. 141–58.
Scott, D.   (2000) 'Plato's critique of the democratic char-
                   acter', in *Phronesis* 45, pp. 19–37.
Taylor, C. C. W.   (1999) 'Plato's totalitarianism', in G. Fine (ed.),
                   Plato 2: Ethics, Politics, Religion and the Soul.

Oxford: Oxford University Press, 1999, pp. 280–96.

Vlastos, G.   (1995) 'Was Plato a feminist?' in his *Studies in Greek Philosophy*, vol. II. Princeton, NJ: Princeton University Press.

White, N.   (1986) 'The rulers' choice', in *Archiv für Geschichte der Philosophie* 68, pp. 22–46.

Williams, B.   (1985) *Ethics and the Limits of Philosophy*. London: Fontana.

(1972) *Morality: an introduction to ethics*. Cambridge: Cambridge University Press.

APPENDIX: GLOSSARY OF GREEK TERMS

akrasia Weakness of will; a phenomenon whereby one acts in accordance with one's non-rational emotions or appetites, contrary to the urgings of reason.

aretē Excellence or virtue.

boulē A council, such as the Athenian Council of Five Hundred.

catharsis Purging; in particular the removal of unwanted emotions or desires from the soul.

dialectic Debate or argument for the sake of finding out the truth.

dianoia Thought; in the *Republic*, a cognitive state primarily associated with mathematical reasoning from assumed principles.

dikaiosunē Justice, the central subject of the *Republic*.

doxa Belief or opinion; in the *Republic*, a cognitive state distinct from knowledge, formed with respect to the sensible, but intrinsically unknowable, realm of physical objects.

dunameis Powers or capacities.

eikasia Imagination; in the *Republic*, the cognitive state associated with perceiving images, either literally or metaphorically – possibly including cases where one is deceived by surface appearances.

ekklēsia An assembly; the democratic *ekklēsia* in Athens, in which all citizens were allowed to participate, was the city's most powerful decision-making institution.

epistemē	Knowledge; in the *Republic*, the cognitive state formed by philosophers with respect to the abstract intelligible realm of Forms.
epithumia	Appetite; the species of motivation pertaining to the third and lowest element of the tripartite soul (the *epithumētikon*). Encompasses physiological urges as well as sexual and more generally materialistic desires (e.g. for wealth).
ergon	Function; often refers to the activity specifically associated with a certain type of object.
eristic	Debate or argument for the sake of victory over one's opponents.
erōs	Can mean love, passion, sexual desire, though in *Republic* IX, it signifies the supremely unjust species of lawless desire associated with the tyrannical soul.
eudaimōn	Possessing *eudaimonia* (see below).
eudaimonia	Happiness, fulfilment, achievement of the 'good' life.
isēgoria	Freedom of speech, a central principle of Athenian democracy.
logos	Reason; the faculty associated with the highest element of the tripartite soul (the *logistikon*), able to motivate pursuit of the good and/or knowledge. The term can also refer to the power of speech, associated with rational agency.
mimēsis	Imitation, for instance 'playing the part' of a fictional character.
noēsis	Understanding; in the *Republic*, the cognitive state corresponding to engagement with abstract Forms or reasoning to first principles (although Plato uses the term inconsistently; see Chapter 3, note 53).
pathē	Feelings or emotions.
phronēsis	Practical wisdom; an intellectual virtue involving the choice of the right ends and means of action.
pistis	Belief; in the *Republic*, a cognitive state formed with respect to actual physical Particulars, as opposed to their images.
polis	A city-state or political community.
prutaneis	Presidents, high-ranking officials.
psuchē	The soul, as possessed by any living organism.

technē   A craft or skill, enabling the successful accomplishment of a given end.

thumos   Spirit; the faculty associated with the second most orderly element of the tripartite soul (the *thumoediēs*), encompassing mental states such as anger, pride, and self-esteem.

NOTES

1. CONTEXT

1 J.A.C.T., *The World of Athens* (1984), p. 157.
2 This is most explicit in Books VI and VII; see section 3.8.4 of this book.

2. OVERVIEW OF THEMES

1 See Aristophanes' *The Clouds* (outlined in section 3.8.4).

3. READING THE TEXT

1 See Julia Annas (1981), pp. 24ff.
2 See R. Cross and A. Woozley (1964), pp. 20ff.
3 Annas (1981), pp. 31–2.
4 Ibid., pp. 30ff.
5 Ibid., p. 36.
6 Cross and Woozley (1964), p. 41.
7 Annas (1981), p. 45.
8 See Cross and Woozley (1964), pp. 51–5, who condemn this argument as 'almost embarrassingly bad' (p. 52).
9 Ibid., p. 56.
10 Annas (1981), p. 53.
11 Ibid., p. 55.
12 Ibid., p. 56.
13 Cross and Woozley (1964), pp. 75–6.
14 Annas (1981), p. 78.
15 One example mentioned is the god Cronos castrating Ouranos with a sickle, and eating his (Cronos') own children.
16 The 'myth of the metals', at (414b) in the text, outlined in section 3.5.1.
17 Annas (1981), p. 96.
18 Admittedly, in Book X, Plato expands his account of the dangers of the arts to include their psychological impact on spectators as well as artists.

19 See Annas (1981), p. 110.
20 Ibid., p. 120.
21 Taylor (1999), p. 293.
22 See, for example, J. S. Mill's position in *On Liberty*.
23 See Rousseau's *The Social Contract* (in particular I, vi–viii and II, iii).
24 Taylor (1999), p. 295.
25 Popper (1995), p. 100.
26 Plato's own pupil Aristotle raised just this question; see his *Politics* (I, V, 1264b15ff.).
27 See Book V (462c–e) for a possible reference to this idea; also Annas (1981, p. 179).
28 See, for instance, Rawls (1973), pp. 180–1.
29 Cross and Woozley (1964), p. 115.
30 See Hume's *A Treatise of Human Nature* (II, iii, 3).
31 See Annas (1981), pp. 133–4.
32 Aristotle (*NE* 1, X) draws an explicit distinction between practical and theoretical elements of reason, which mirrors this implicit distinction in Plato; see section 4.1.
33 See Book VII of Aristotle's *Nicomachean Ethics*, and for a seminal twentieth-century treatment Davidson (1980).
34 Annas (1981), p. 128.
35 See Cooper (1984), pp. 15–16 on this problem.
36 See also Annas (1981), p. 138.
37 For Aristotle's taxonomy of virtues see, for instance, the *Nicomachean Ethics*, Books II–V. For his accounts of the various emotions see *Rhetoric* Book II.
38 Sachs (1963), p. 141.
39 See Annas' (1981) distinction between act-centred and agent-centred ethical theories, pp. 157ff.
40 See N. O. Dahl, in G. Fine (eds) (1999), pp. 218–19.
41 See Plato's *Phaedo* (60a).
42 Vlastos (1995), pp. 134–5.
43 Annas (1976), pp. 309ff.
44 Annas (1981), pp. 311ff.
45 Vlastos (1995), p. 133.
46 For an early version of this argument see Aristotle's *Politics* (1262b15, ff.).
47 For a possible answer, see Vlastos (1995), pp. 138–9.
48 Cross and Woozley (1964), pp. 145ff.
49 Annas (1981), pp. 195ff.
50 Ibid., p. 209.
51 Harrison (1993), p. 156.
52 Ibid., pp. 158–9.
53 Later (at 533e), when this fourfold division is repeated, the term applied to subsection 1 changes from understanding (*noēsis*) to knowledge (*epistemē*). Rather confusingly, moreover, understanding (*noēsis*) is here used to refer to knowledge (*epistemē*) and thought (*dianoia*) taken together; i.e. to refer collectively to the cognitive states aroused by the intelligible sphere (section A of the line).

54 Annas (1981), p. 250.
55 Cross and Woozley (1964), p. 220.
56 See (595a, ff.); for further discussion of this passage see section 3.12.1.
57 In the passage of text (537d–539d).
58 See (516e–517a), (517d–e), (520b–c), (539e).
59 See also (519e).
60 White (1986), pp. 22ff.
61 Reeve (1988), pp. 202–3.
62 Kraut (1991), pp. 245ff.
63 Ibid., p. 247.
64 See Annas (1981), pp. 301–2.
65 Scott (2000), pp. 27ff.
66 Ibid., p. 26.
67 Annas (1981), p. 304.
68 Cross and Woozley (1964), pp. 265–6.
69 Ibid., p. 267.
70 See (377d–389c); also section 3.4.1 of this book.
71 Plato raises other arguments for the soul's immortality in the *Phaedo* (beginning 70c). In the *Apology* (40c–e) however, Socrates seems to acknowledge the possibility that bodily death could be the end of conscious experience.
72 Annas (1981), p. 345.

4. RECEPTION AND INFLUENCE

1 A reference to *Republic* (420c) or (519e).
2 Issues arising from this point were discussed in section 3.5.3.
3 See also (1181a1ff.)
4 Popper (1995), p. 102.
5 Ibid., p. 86.
6 Ibid., p. 98.
7 Ibid., p. 86.
8 Ibid., p. 107.
9 See Taylor (1999).
10 *On Liberty*, passim.
11 See section 3.7.1.
12 Crossman (1959), pp. 141ff.
13 Acton (1938), pp. 303ff.
14 Ibid., p. 307.
15 See their works listed in the bibliography: MacIntyre (1981), Foot (1978), Williams (1985).
16 Annas (1981), pp. 157ff.
17 Williams (1972), pp. 13ff.
18 Nagel (1970), pp. 3ff.

INDEX

Printed in Great Britain
by Amazon